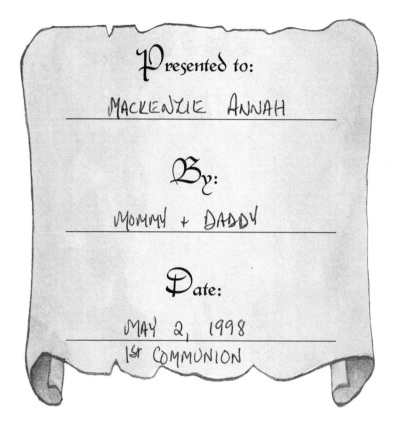

Presented to:

MACKENZIE ANNAH

By:

MOMMY + DADDY

Date:

MAY 2, 1998

1st COMMUNION

FACE-TO-FACE
WITH
Women of the Bible

Face-to-Face
WITH
Women of the Bible

NANCY SIMPSON

Illustrated by
DREW AND NANCY WARD

CHARIOT
VICTOR
PUBLISHING
A DIVISION OF COOK COMMUNICATIONS

Chariot Books™ is an imprint of Chariot • Victor Publishing
Cook Communications, Colorado Springs, Colorado 80918
Cook Communications, Paris, Ontario
Kingsway Communications, Eastbourne, England

FACE-TO-FACE WITH WOMEN OF THE BIBLE
© 1996 by Cook Communications for text and Drew and Nancy Ward for illustrations.

Cover and interior design by Paetzold Design, Batavia, IL

Illustrations by Drew and Nancy Ward

Verses marked (TLB) are taken from *The Living Bible* © 1971, owned by assignment by Illinois Regional Bank N.A.
(as trustee). Used by permission of Tyndale House Publishers Inc., Wheaton, IL 60189. All rights reserved.

Verses marked (NASB) are taken from the *New American Standard Bible*, © The Lockman Foundation 1960, 1962,
1963, 1968, 1971, 1972, 1973, 1975, 1977. Used by permission.

First printing, 1996
Printed in Canada
00 99 98 97 96   5 4 3 2 1

ISBN 0-7814-0251-4

Introduction

$\mathcal{I}$n this book you will read about women who chose to follow God, women who were courageous even in the face of great danger to themselves, their families, and their people. You will read about women who accepted God's challenge and became great heroines. Some of these women will be familiar to you, such as Ruth, Esther, and Mary. But other names you may not recognize—Shiphrah and Puah, Jehosheba, and Phoebe.

Not all of the women you'll read about in this book chose to follow God. Look at their lives carefully to see what happened because of their bad choices. All of us can learn to make good choices in our walk with God by seeing the mistakes of others.

The women in this book are not just good women or bad women. But, like you, they were once young, and made both good and bad decisions as they grew up. They had to decide to choose God's way or their own way. They didn't always make the right choices, just as you won't always make the right choices. But the difference in whether they became women of God or not is what they did about their failures and successes.

All the stories in this book are in the same order as they appear in your Bible and give the Bible book and chapter number of where the story can be found. You will also see the phonetic spellings of difficult names to help you pronounce them correctly. And, at the end of the book, you will find a chart with the meanings of many of the Bible names you read about.

Now, relax, get comfortable, and open your heart while you read these exciting stories about women who served God with their lives in a big way!

Contents

OLD TESTAMENT

NEW TESTAMENT

Women of the
Old Testament

Eve

FIRST WOMAN IN CREATION

Genesis 3

'M HUNGRY!" Adam suddenly declared. He and Eve had been swimming in the frosty cold water of the rock pool the Lord God had made just for them. They dove deep, but could not touch the bottom of the pool. It was a game they played and it made the Lord God laugh.

"I'm hungry too," Eve gasped as her head popped above the water.

They raced to the center of the garden where God had planted trees of every kind. Eve rolled her eyes as she watched Adam pluck juicy fruit from the trees.

"You know, the best-looking apples are over there on that tree," Eve said, pointing to a giant of a tree loaded with the biggest apples in the garden.

"That's the Tree of Conscience," Adam replied. "The Lord God said not to eat apples from that tree. He said eating its fruit would make you aware of good and evil, and you would be doomed to die!"

"Yes, I remember what He said," Eve said.

Eve, still curious, walked closer to the Tree of Conscience. Why would God plant such a tree if no one could eat from it? Eve inspected the ground

under the tree. Unlike the other trees, no leaves had fallen and neither had any overripe fruit. It was as if the same apples remained permanently on the branches.

"That's odd," she said out loud.

"That's odd, indeed," said a voice from behind the tree. It was a funny nasal-sounding voice with a hiss.

Eve stared as slowly a long skinny creature emerged, winding itself around the tree's trunk. It turned and twisted into loops and bumps until it was impossible to tell which was the creature's top and which was its bottom.

"Oh, hi, Serpent," said Eve with a sniff. She really didn't care for Serpent.

"Don't tie yourself into a knot!" Eve laughed.

"Hmmpf!" Serpent spat. He looked straight at Eve, his round eyes focused.

"You are very intelligent, young lady, to notice that the fruit from the Tree of Conscience is different from that of other trees," Serpent flattered Eve. "This is the best fruit in the garden. Try a piece!"

"No, God says we can't eat fruit from this tree! He says we will know good from bad, and will be doomed to die. Excuse me, what does it mean to die?"

"It means nothing to die," hissed Serpent. "God was telling a lie. He knows that if you eat the fruit from the Tree of Conscience, you will become like Him. You will be wise and able to distinguish good from evil."

Eve looked at the serpent. She did so want to be wise like the Lord God and know the answers to all of her questions. She had so many of them.

"Here, just try one of these beautiful apples," Serpent tempted again. "Surely, it won't hurt to try just one."

Adam strolled over to see who Eve was talking to.

"Okay," Eve gave in. She plucked an apple off the tree and held it gingerly in her hands. Nothing bad happened.

"See, there is no danger," cooed Serpent. "Go ahead, take a bite."

Eve held the apple to her lips and bit into it.

"Delicious!" she exclaimed, wiping the juice that rolled down her chin. She

14

passed it to Adam and he also took a bite. Then, they hurriedly ate the entire apple. "Oh, I feel strange," Eve said.

"Me too," Adam said as he rubbed his stomach.

"Maybe it was a bad idea to eat that apple after all," Eve said, then gasped at her words. Now she understood the difference between good and bad.

"We're in trouble now! We better hide so the Lord God won't find out what we did!" Adam exclaimed. He pulled Eve behind a bush just as heavy footsteps were heard entering the garden.

"Why are you hiding from Me?" God asked, immediately spotting Adam and Eve's hiding place. "Have you eaten fruit from the Tree of Conscience?"

"Yes," Adam answered the Lord, "but it was Eve's fault. She ate it first and then gave it to me!"

Eve frowned at Adam. Why did he try to pass all the blame to her? After all, he had been free to refuse to eat the fruit.

"Even though you, a woman, will be blamed for eating the fruit first," God said, "one day, through a woman, a Savior will be born who will save all His people from evil.

"Because you both disobeyed Me and ate the fruit from the Tree of Conscience, you will have to leave the garden," God told them sadly. "Many hardships will come upon you, but don't fear, I will always be with you."

As a loving father, God always has a plan to help us when we make bad choices.

[God] sent his Son, born of a woman . . .
to buy freedom for us . . . so that he could
adopt us as his very own [children].
GALATIANS 4:4, 5, TLB

Sarah

PRINCESS GOD DID NOT FORGET

GENESIS 15, 16, 17, 18, 21

EARS FLOWED DOWN SARAI'S (SAIR-eyes) FACE. "Lord God," Sarai cried, "Please let me become pregnant and have a baby." She had longed all her life to be a mother and have a baby all her own. She had prayed many times, asking God for a child. But even as she asked now, she knew that she was too old to have a baby. Sarai was past seventy years old!

Ten years ago, God had promised Sarai's husband, Abram, that he would become the father of a great nation; that he would have a son to inherit the family name. Indeed, God had told Abram that his descendants would be as the stars above—too many to count!

"I am Abram's wife," Sarah reminded God. "How can he have children except through me?"

It was then that she caught sight of her Egyptian maid. Hagar (HAY-garr) was walking down the path to the well, a large pitcher balanced atop her head. She was young and healthy. Suddenly, Sarai had a plan.

"Since the Lord has given me no children," Sarai told Abram that evening. "You can take my maid, Hagar, as your second wife and the children she has

16

will be counted as mine."

Abram took Hagar as his second wife and she became pregnant. Hagar was very proud of her pregnancy and believed she was better than Sarai. She made fun of Sarai and teased her. Sarai was heartbroken.

Finally, Sarai could stand it no longer. She beat Hagar and the maid ran away. But the angel of the Lord came to Hagar and said, "Return to your mistress, Sarai, and act as you should, for I will make you into a great nation. Your baby will be a son and you should name him *Ishmael* (ISH-me-uhl), which means 'God hears,' for God has heard your cries."

Hagar returned to Sarai's tent and the baby, Ishmael, was born. Sarai tried hard to accept Ishmael as her own child, but deep inside, she knew it wasn't so. She wished she could have had her own children to love. It looked as if God's promise to give Abram as many descendants as the stars would be fulfilled through Hagar and not through Sarai.

One day Abram burst into the tent. "The Lord just told me some amazing things!" he told Sarai excitedly. "He changed my name to *Abraham*, meaning 'father of nations,' and said I will have millions of descendants who will form many nations. Then, He changed your name to *Sarah*, meaning 'Princess' and said you will have a son and will be the mother of nations. Many kings will come from you!"

Sarai gasped! She was almost ninety years old! Could this be possible? Had Abram been out in the sun too long? Nevertheless, she changed her name to Sarah, while he changed his to Abraham.

Soon afterwards, the Lord visited Abraham and Sarah's tent. "Next year, I will give you and Sarah a son," He told Abraham.

Sarah laughed silently. "I am too old and so is Abraham to have a baby," she chuckled to herself.

"Why did Sarah laugh?" God asked, for He could hear her silent laughter even when Abraham could not. "Is anything too hard for God? Next year, just as I told you, Sarah will have a son!"

God did as He promised. Sarah became pregnant and had a baby son. She named the baby *Isaac* meaning "laughter."

"God has brought me laughter!" Sarah declared. "All who hear about this shall rejoice with me. For who would have dreamed that I could have a baby? Yet, I have given Abraham a child in his old age!"

Isaac became the child of promise, through whose line was born the nation of Israel. Sarah learned that the promise to Abraham was also meant for her; for, indeed, she became the mother of a line of kings that ended with the birth of Jesus, the King of Kings.

Believe in God's promises and He will count you as righteous.

God will accept us in the same way he accepted Abraham—when we believe the promises of God. . . .
ROMANS 4:24, TLB

Hagar

SLAVE WHO FOUND MERCY

GENESIS 21:8-19

ET RID OF THAT SLAVE GIRL and her son!" Sarah told her husband, Abraham, after she caught Ishmael (ISH-me-uhl) teasing her own son, Isaac. "Ishmael is not going to share your possessions with my son, Isaac. I won't have it!"

Abraham was upset at Sarah's words. He did not want to send away his son, Ishmael. Ishmael's mother, Hagar (HAY-garr), was Sarah's Egyptian slave. Sarah had given Hagar to Abraham as a second wife when Sarah believed she could have no children. She wanted Hagar to have children by Abraham so that Sarah could call them her own. But through a miracle from God, Sarah had become pregnant and had given Abraham a son, Isaac. The boys were half brothers; each had the same father, but different mothers.

"O God, what shall I do?" Abraham asked the Lord.

"Do as Sarah says and don't worry about Ishmael and Hagar," the Lord answered. "I will bless them and cause a nation to come from Ishmael."

The next morning, Hagar looked up into the face of Abraham with tear-stained eyes. Had he really told her to leave the only family she had known?

Hagar felt the weight of the food and water that Abraham had strapped to her back. Unable to speak a word, she gripped her son's hand fearfully.

"Don't be afraid," Abraham told her. "God will be with you." He gently pushed her away from the tent toward the open wilderness.

Panic took hold of Hagar. "Please don't send us away!" she begged.

"You must go. You can no longer live in Sarah's tent," Abraham replied.

Seeing that further words were useless, Hagar turned and led her son out into the wilderness of Beersheba. It was hot and dry. Hagar and Ishmael wandered aimlessly. *Which direction shall I go?* she asked herself helplessly.

Soon the water that Hagar carried was gone. Ishmael became faint and staggered. Hagar soon had to lay him down in the shade of a bush. Overcome with grief, she said aloud, "I can't watch him die!"

Suddenly, a voice called to her. "Hagar, don't be afraid! God has heard the boy's cries. Go and get him, for I will make of him a great nation."

Hagar stood, her tears turning to joy. God had spoken to her! She had hope and a promise for the future. Hagar turned and noticed a well of water standing not far from her. She ran to it and filled her water skin with the cool water; then she ran to give Ishmael a drink.

Ishmael grew up in the wilderness. He became an expert archer. Hagar arranged a marriage for him with an Egyptian girl. Through her son and his children, Hagar became the foundress of the Arab peoples.

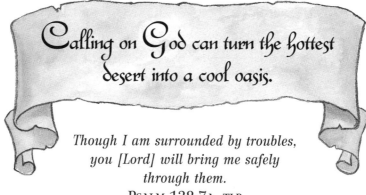

Calling on God can turn the hottest desert into a cool oasis.

Though I am surrounded by troubles, you [Lord] will bring me safely through them.
PSALM 138:7A, TLB

Deborah
the Nurse
WITNESS OF FAITH AND TRUST

GENESIS 24:1-67; 35:8

 AM OLD, almost one hundred years of age! In Hebrew households, the old women tell stories, not only to amuse the children but also to preserve our history. It is a very important job! But I wasn't always a storyteller. Many years ago I was a servant in the house of Bethuel, a relative of Abraham. My primary responsibility was to be a nurse for young Rebekah, Bethuel's daughter. She was such a delightful child. I enjoyed watching her grow to become a beautiful young woman. I have seen many things in my one hundred years, but nothing to equal Rebekah's faith and trust. When she was just sixteen, she left her family home and set out to follow a stranger to a faraway land to marry a husband she had never met. I went with her on that unusual journey.

Let me tell you all about it . . .

One evening, long ago, a stranger came to our village. He was a servant sent by Abraham to find a suitable girl to marry his son, Isaac. The far-off land where Abraham's family lived was inhabited by Canaanites and there were no Hebrew girls for Isaac to marry.

The servant had stopped his camels beside a spring of water to wait for the girls of our village to come to fill their water pitchers.

"Oh Lord," Abraham's servant prayed, "show me which girl I should choose to be Isaac's wife. When I ask one of them for a drink, let her say, 'Yes, certainly, and I will draw water for your camels, too.' Then, I will know she is the one you have appointed as Isaac's wife."

As he was praying, my beautiful young Rebekah arrived at the spring to fill her pitcher. Running to her, Abraham's servant asked for a drink.

"Certainly, sir," Rebekah had answered, giving him a drink. Then, she said, "I'll draw water for your camels too."

After she had finished the task, the servant gave her some gold jewelry. Then he asked, "Whose daughter are you?"

"My father is Bethuel," Rebekah had replied.

The servant stood amazed. God had led him to a girl from the family of Abraham's own brother! The servant followed Rebekah home and explained everything to Rebekah's father, Bethuel.

"Obviously, the Lord has sent you here," said Bethuel. "Let Rebekah be the wife of Abraham's son, as the Lord God has directed."

Abraham's servant fell to his knees at this reply, overcome with thanksgiving for the Lord's direction. Then the servant brought out gold and silver for Rebekah and lovely clothing and presents for her family.

They were such fine gifts. My Rebekah looked so beautiful.

Her family made preparations for Rebekah to journey to Abraham's home where she would marry Isaac. Rebekah's servants, myself included, were to go with her. We hurried as we only had a few days to get things in order. Imagine our surprise when the next morning, Abraham's servant insisted upon leaving that very day!

"But we want to keep Rebekah here at least another ten days!" her mother had exclaimed. But the servant insisted upon going immediately.

"I will go today," Rebekah had decided upon hearing the matter. She and we servants set out on camels to journey to a place never before seen. We were to become a part of a family we had never known. I must confess that we servants were a bit nervous, but Rebekah was not worried. She followed Abraham's servant willingly, knowing it was God who guided him.

We finally arrived at the tents of Abraham where Isaac made Rebekah his wife. He loved her very much and she loved him. I continued to serve

Rebekah and when, after twenty years of waiting, she finally had children, I took care of her twin boys, Jacob and Esau. I grew to love the family of Abraham and Sarah, Isaac and Rebekah, and was glad that Rebekah had the courage and the faith to follow the Lord God's leading.

God has a plan for your life.
Ask Him and He will make it clear.

I will instruct you (says the Lord)
and guide you along the best
pathway for your life.
PSALM 32:8A TLB

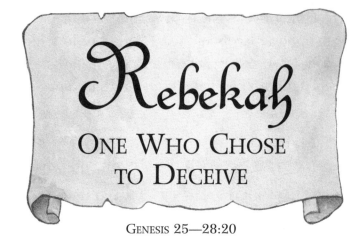

Rebekah

ONE WHO CHOSE
TO DECEIVE

GENESIS 25—28:20

I MUST DO SOMETHING to keep Isaac from giving his oldest son, Esau, the blessing. Jacob is the one who is supposed to be blessed!" Rebekah said as she hurried to find her son, Jacob. A plan, that's what she needed.

When Rebekah was pregnant with her twin boys, Esau and Jacob, the Lord had told her that the older one (the one born first) would be a servant to the younger one (the one born second). Esau was born first, and Jacob was born second with his hand on Esau's heel.

Esau, a strong, loud boy who liked to hunt, was Isaac's favorite. Jacob, a quiet, studious boy, was Rebekah's favorite. She knew God wanted to keep His promise of a Hebrew nation through the descendants of Jacob, not Esau.

Esau had sold his birthright—the right of the oldest son in the family to inherit family position and wealth. He had sold it to Jacob for a bowl of stew! Esau had also married two Hittite girls, defying God's warning to marry only Hebrew wives.

Rebekah's husband, Isaac, would not admit to the flaws in Esau. This morning, Isaac, now old and blind, had told Esau to go hunting and bring

him some venison cooked just the way he liked it. Then, Isaac would give Esau a blessing before he died.

"Bring me two young goats and I'll fix your father's favorite stew," Rebekah told Jacob quickly. There was no time to waste. "You can pretend to be Esau and take the dish to Isaac. He will give his blessings to you instead of Esau."

"But, Mother, Esau is more hairy than I am. If Father feels my hands, he will know I am not Esau," Jacob pointed out.

"I will make you gloves from hairy goatskin and a strip of goatskin to go around your neck. You can also wear Esau's clothing. Everything will work out. You don't have to worry."

Rebekah cooked the goats and Jacob carried the dish to his father.

"Who are you, my son, Esau or Jacob?" blind Isaac asked.

"I am Esau," Jacob lied. "Eat your stew so you can bless me."

"Let me feel you," said Isaac. He felt Jacob's hands covered with goatskin. *It is Jacob's voice, but Esau's hands,* Isaac thought.

"Are you really Esau?" Isaac asked out loud.

"Yes," replied Jacob.

"Then bring me the venison and I will eat it and bless you."

After Isaac ate the stew, he gave Jacob the oldest son's blessing.

As soon as Jacob left the room, Esau brought a bowl of venison stew to his father. "Here I am, Father. Eat your stew so you can bless me."

"What?" Isaac gasped. "Who is it?"

"It's me, Esau, your oldest son."

"Your brother was here and tricked me. I gave your blessing to him. I have no other blessing to give you," Isaac sadly replied.

Then Esau became very angry and decided to kill Jacob.

"Flee to your Uncle Laban's house in Haran," Rebekah told Jacob.

Isaac told Jacob to do as his mother said. "May God pass on to you and your descendants the blessing promised to Abraham," Isaac continued.

On his journey, Jacob had a vision. God told him that he was God's choice and that through Jacob, the promises to Abraham would be fulfilled.

Just as God had foretold, Jacob became the head of the family. His mother, Rebekah, had the right idea wanting to help Jacob reach his rightful place in the family. However, she worked out a lie to get what God had promised. Doing the wrong thing for the right reason is not the same as obeying God and letting Him fulfill His promise. We will never know how God could have changed the circumstances without Rebekah's choosing to deceive her husband.

As for Esau, he married a third wife, a daughter of Ishmael, founder of the Arab nation.

Following God's direction makes things work out right.

I delight to do your will,
my God, for your law is written
upon my heart!
PSALM 40:8, TLB

Rachel

WOMAN WHO LEARNED TO WAIT

GENESIS 29:1-30

 ACHEL moved through the open field of grass, keeping pace with the flock of sheep that hurried to the well. It was watering time and the sheep knew it. Rachel was thirsty herself. Shepherding sheep was hot and tiring work.

Gazing ahead, Rachel saw that other flocks of sheep had reached the well ahead of hers. Good! She would not have to wait. It was customary for shepherds to wait until all the flocks and shepherds had arrived before removing the heavy stone cover from the well.

As she approached the well, Rachel was surprised to see a stranger. *He looks as though he has traveled a great distance,* she told herself. *His robes and sandals are dusty and travel-stained. Oh! See how handsome he is and how young!*

Although Rachel was very beautiful (her family and friends often had told her so), she wished she were dressed in something finer than shepherd's robes and smelled of something better than sheep!

"Please allow me to water your flock of sheep," the stranger offered Rachel. She liked his warm voice and the cheerful glint in his eyes.

She nodded and as the man helped her, a shiver ran through her whenever their eyes chanced to meet. When the task was done, the man said, "I am Jacob, the son of your Aunt Rebekah, your father's sister." Then he kissed her cheek and she noticed tears in his eyes.

Rachel ran quickly to her father, Laban, who rushed to meet Jacob and invited him to stay at their house. Jacob stayed with Rachel's family for some time. He worked with her father and brothers in the fields. Finally, Laban said to him, "Just because we are relatives is no reason for you to work for me without pay. How much do you want?"

By this time, Jacob had fallen deeply in love with Rachel. "I'll work for you for seven years if you'll give me Rachel as my wife."

Laban agreed.

Rachel was overjoyed. Her heart raced with excitement thinking about being the wife of such a loving, handsome man. Seven years would seem but a few days. She could wait. She and Jacob were so much in love.

But the news made someone in Rachel's family very sad—her older sister, Leah. She was not beautiful like Rachel and no one wanted to marry her.

Seven years passed quickly. Rachel could hardly wait as the big day approached. But then, on the very day of her wedding, a most shameful thing happened. Rachel's father forced Rachel to stay hidden at home, while her sister, Leah, put on the traditional wedding veils. When it was dark, Laban brought Leah to him, heavily veiled. Jacob, thinking it was Rachel, slept with Leah, making her his wife.

Alone, in her own bed, Rachel's tears flowed as she wondered what Jacob would do the next morning when he discovered the trick her father had played on him. Would Jacob be so angry that he would leave all of them forever, including Rachel? She could not bear the thought.

"Please let Jacob still love me tomorrow," she prayed to the Lord.

The next morning, Jacob was angry. Rachel listened as he yelled angrily at Laban. "How could you trick me like this? I worked seven years for Rachel!"

"I could not marry off a younger daughter ahead of her older sister," Laban replied. "You can marry Rachel, too, if you promise to work for me for another seven years!" (In those days, a lot of men took more than one wife.)

Rachel held her breath. Would Jacob agree to this? Did Jacob love her enough to work seven additional years after he had been tricked so cruelly? This would, indeed, be a test of his love.

"Okay," she heard Jacob quietly agree. "I will do as you say."

Rachel's heart leapt with joy. "Thank You!" she cried to God. Jacob truly loved her. Their love would be more precious because of the hardships they had to endure to see it happen.

Working hard for something can make it more valuable.

[Love] bears all things, believes all things, hopes all things, endures all things. Love never fails.
I Corinthians 13:7,8a, NASB

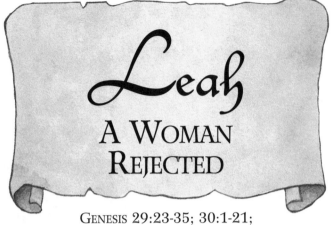

Leah
A WOMAN REJECTED

GENESIS 29:23-35; 30:1-21;
MATTHEW 1:2, 3

"MY FIRST SON shall be named *Reuben*, meaning 'behold a son,' because God has looked favorably upon me," Leah declared, happily. Surely, her husband, Jacob, would love her now that she had given him a son.

The first years of marriage had been hard for Leah. Jacob paid little attention to her, giving all of his love to his second wife, Leah's younger sister. Rachel was far prettier than Leah. Jacob had only married Leah because he had been tricked into the marriage by Laban, their father.

"O Lord, please let Jacob love me too, just a little," Leah had prayed sadly. Although the Lord did not make Jacob love her, He had given Leah a beautiful child while Rachel remained unable to bear children.

Although Jacob was pleased with Leah's son, his love for her did not increase. Again, God answered Leah's pleas by giving her a second son which she named *Simeon*, meaning "The Lord heard." She said, "The Lord heard that I was unloved and so He has given me another son."

God then gave her another son which she named *Levi*, meaning "attachment." *Surely, now my husband will love me since I have given him three sons,*

34

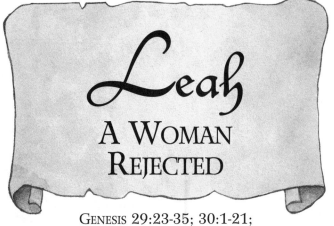

Leah

A WOMAN REJECTED

GENESIS 29:23-35; 30:1-21;
MATTHEW 1:2, 3

MY FIRST SON shall be named *Reuben*, meaning 'behold a son,' because God has looked favorably upon me," Leah declared, happily. Surely, her husband, Jacob, would love her now that she had given him a son.

The first years of marriage had been hard for Leah. Jacob paid little attention to her, giving all of his love to his second wife, Leah's younger sister. Rachel was far prettier than Leah. Jacob had only married Leah because he had been tricked into the marriage by Laban, their father.

"O Lord, please let Jacob love me too, just a little," Leah had prayed sadly. Although the Lord did not make Jacob love her, He had given Leah a beautiful child while Rachel remained unable to bear children.

Although Jacob was pleased with Leah's son, his love for her did not increase. Again, God answered Leah's pleas by giving her a second son which she named *Simeon*, meaning "The Lord heard." She said, "The Lord heard that I was unloved and so He has given me another son."

God then gave her another son which she named *Levi*, meaning "attachment." *Surely, now my husband will love me since I have given him three sons,*

Leah hoped, but she was again disappointed. Jacob loved only Rachel.

Leah had another son. She named him *Judah*, meaning "praise." "Now I will praise the Lord God!" she declared, knowing that even though she would never receive the love that Jacob showed her younger sister, she had received love and attention from the Lord. She looked to the Lord for the love she missed from her husband.

Meanwhile, Rachel had not had any children herself and became increasingly jealous of Leah's children. Finally, she told Jacob to sleep with her maid, Bilhah, so that Bilhah's children would become Rachel's.

Bilhah became pregnant and had a son that Rachel named *Dan*, meaning "justice," for Rachel said, "God has been just and has given me a son too." Then, Bilhah again became pregnant with another son that Rachel named *Naphtali*, meaning "struggle." She said, "I am in a fierce contest with my sister, and I am catching up!"

Leah then realized that she was not getting pregnant anymore. *My four sons are the only things that Jacob loves about me,* she thought frantically. So she let Jacob sleep with her maid, Zilpah. Soon Zilpah had a son that Leah named *Gad*, meaning "my luck has turned," and then another son whom Leah named *Asher*, meaning "happy." Leah said, "What joy is mine!"

Then, to show the world that love should not be based on outer beauty, but on beauty of the heart, God gave Leah two more sons named *Issachar* and *Zebulun* and a daughter named Dinah. He also added Leah and her son, Judah, to the line through whom His own Son was born—Jesus!

Lasting beauty is found only on the inside of a person.

Man looks at the outward appearance, but the Lord looks at the heart.
I SAMUEL 16:7B, NASB

Tamar

PURSUER OF JUSTICE

GENESIS 38:6-30; MATTHEW 1:3

AMAR WAS NOT SORRY that her husband, Er, was dead. Er had been a cruel man and most people said that God had killed him for his wickedness. Tamar was sad, however, that she had no children. Now, she might never be a mother!

"My second son, Onan, will marry you, as Jewish law requires of a dead man's brother," Judah, Er's father told Tamar. "That way, the children that you have by Onan will count as Er's children."

Tamar's face lit up. She would now marry Onan and have children! But again, Tamar was disappointed. Onan refused to father any children that would not be counted as his own.

Soon Onan also died. All the people were shocked and said that God had killed him because he had refused to give Tamar any children.

"Return to your parents' home and wait until my youngest son, Shelah, is old enough to marry you," Judah told Tamar.

Tamar went to live with her parents; but when Shelah was grown, Judah did not marry him to Tamar. He was afraid Shelah might also die.

36

Tamar wondered what to do. She knew that Jewish law required the father-in-law to marry the widow of his son if he had no other sons to marry her so that children would be born to carry on the family name. If Judah did not give his son, Shelah, to Tamar to marry, then it was Judah's duty to father Tamar's children. Judah refused, but upon learning that Judah was traveling to the city of Timnah, Tamar devised a plan.

I will trick Judah into fulfilling his duty, Tamar said to herself with delight. And he won't even know he's doing it.

After disguising herself with a long veil, Tamar hurried to sit beside the road at the entrance to the city of Enaim, which was on the way to Timnah. Soon Judah walked by. He noticed Tamar sitting beside the road and thought she was a prostitute. He promised to pay her a young goat if she would sleep with him. She asked him to give her his walking stick and identification seal as a pledge of payment. Judah slept with Tamar and she became pregnant with his child.

Afterward, Judah went on to Timnah and Tamar hurried home. Later, when Judah tried to get back his walking stick and identification seal, he could not find the prostitute anywhere.

Three months later, Judah heard that Tamar was pregnant. He became angry and thought she had become a prostitute. A prostitute slept with men for money. "Bring her out and burn her!" he cried.

As the men were dragging her out of her house to kill her, Tamar called out, "The man who owns this identification seal and walking stick is the father of my child!"

Then Judah, seeing his own seal and stick, knew what had happened. "Tamar was more in the right than me," he admitted. "I refused to keep my promise to give her my son, Shelah, in marriage."

Tamar was allowed to live although Judah refused to marry her. Soon afterward, Tamar gave birth to twin boys. As they were being born, the midwife tied a scarlet thread around the wrist of the baby who appeared first, but he drew back and the other baby was the first to be born. He was named *Perez* which means "bursting out" and his brother was named *Zerah*.

God honored Tamar, the Gentile woman, who underwent humiliation in her attempt to produce heirs for the family of Judah; for it was through Tamar and her son, Perez, that the family line continued on to the birth of Jesus. Little did Judah know that he almost burned to death an ancestor of God's own Son!

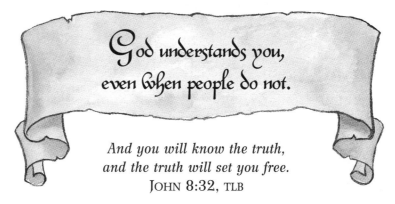

God understands you,
even when people do not.

*And you will know the truth,
and the truth will set you free.*
JOHN 8:32, TLB

Shiphrah and Puah

SERVANTS AT PERIL BEFORE PHARAOH

EXODUS 1:15-21

RING IN THE MIDWIVES, Shiphrah (SHIFF-ruh) and Puah (PEW-uh)!" Pharaoh, King of Egypt, ordered.

Trembling, the two women stood before Pharaoh.

"When you deliver Hebrew babies, I want you to kill every boy!" Pharaoh instructed them.

"Yes, Sire," the women replied and left as quickly as possible.

"What should we do?" Shiphrah wailed as soon as they were safely outside the palace. "If we kill the babies, we will be acting against God, but if we let them live, we will disobey Pharaoh and he will kill us!"

The women stared at each other in dismay. They loved the Hebrew God and did not want to hurt His people. Still, they were very afraid of Pharaoh. Pharaoh hated the Hebrews. He believed they were becoming too numerous and did not want any more Hebrew boys to be born.

Shiphrah and Puah were midwives. They helped pregnant mothers birth their babies and helped to care for them afterward.

40

"There may be a way out of this," Puah suggested. "We let the Hebrew boy babies live and if Pharaoh finds out, we tell him the Hebrew women don't call us until it's already too late and their babies have come."

"That's a good idea," Shiphrah agreed. So the midwives did not carry out Pharaoh's order and the Hebrew male babies were allowed to live.

It wasn't long before the midwives were again called before Pharaoh. "Why have you disobeyed me and let the Hebrew baby boys live?" he demanded.

"Sire," Shiphrah and Puah answered, "the Hebrew mothers have their babies so quickly that we cannot get to them in time! They are much different than the Egyptian women who take their time delivering babies."

Pharaoh believed Shiphrah and Puah. He did not press his order further and the people of Israel continued to multiply. Shiphrah and Puah, who had risked their own lives to save Hebrew infants, were blessed by God for their courage and faith. He rewarded them by giving them children of their own.

Following God's commands instead of man's commands brings godly protection and reward.

We must obey God rather than men.
ACTS 5:29, TLB

Jochebed
MOTHER WHO TRUSTED GOD

EXODUS 2:1-10; 6:20;
NUMBERS 26:59; HEBREWS 11:23

OCHEBED (JOCK-uh-bed) CAREFULLY rocked her baby boy to sleep. "Hush, hush, little baby," she said as she lovingly rubbed his tiny hand.

She knew if the Egyptians heard him cry, they would kill him! The Hebrew population had multiplied too fast for the Egyptians, so Pharaoh had ordered all Hebrew baby boys to be drowned in the Nile River. They feared the Hebrews might one day fight against them.

Sighing heavily, Jochebed wished the Hebrews had not moved to Egypt. She wished they would have stayed in the land of Canaan, the land promised to Abraham by God. Jochebed was a daughter of Levi, one of the twelve sons of Jacob who had moved to Egypt to escape a famine. But now they had become slaves to the Egyptians.

"I can no longer hide you in this little house, my son," Jochebed whispered to the sleeping baby. "You are getting too big. Soon, someone will find out you are here."

Jochebed was determined to save her baby. She had always been a woman of great faith. Even her name meant "glory of the Lord."

Jochebed placed her sleeping baby into a woven basket made of reeds. She had waterproofed the basket with tar. Carrying the basket to the river, Jochebed closed the basket lid, whispered a prayer, and laid it among the reeds along the river's edge.

"Miriam," Jochebed addressed her ten-year-old daughter, "stay close by and watch what happens to the basket."

With a heavy heart, Jochebed returned home. She had done all she could for her baby. She could not stay among the reeds to watch the baby's basket, but she knew her young daughter, Miriam, would do her best.

"Dear God," Jochebed prayed, "please take care of Miriam and the baby!" Kneeling beside her bed, Jochebed left it all in God's hands.

Trusting in the Lord when we are afraid gives us new hope.

*Yes, Lord, let your constant love
surround us, for our hopes
are in you alone.*
PSALM 33:22, TLB

Miriam

YOUNG GUARDIAN OF A PROPHET

EXODUS 2:1-10; 15:20, 21

HIDDEN AMONG the tall reeds of the riverbank, Miriam watched anxiously as the small basket bobbed gently in the shallow water at the river's edge. The baby inside the basket was her own little brother. His very life was threatened by a cruel Egyptian law that called for the death of every newborn Hebrew boy.

Miriam's mother, Jochebed, had hidden her baby boy until he was too big to hide anymore. Then she had waterproofed a basket made of reeds and had laid her son in it. Miriam helped her mother get the basket ready. When it was completed, Miriam walked beside her mother to a sheltered part of the Nile River, a place close to the women's quarters of the great palace of Pharaoh.

Jochebed had lowered the basket into the water. "It is now up to you to keep watch, Miriam, and to tell me what happens to him. May the Lord God take care of him and you."

Ten-year-old Miriam kept watch faithfully. It was hot and sticky among the reeds and insects bit her unceasingly. She was thirsty and wished for a cool spot to rest. But she did not give up her post.

Suddenly, Miriam's ears heard a sound. She crouched lower behind the reeds. Someone was coming!

Peeking out ever so carefully, Miriam saw a beautiful young woman coming towards the river from the direction of the palace. It was a princess, one of Pharaoh's own daughters. She and her maids were heading right to the spot where the basket floated!

"That basket bobs low in the water," the princess said. "Bring it to me," she commanded a servant.

Miriam watched fearfully as the servant carried the basket to the princess. Soon she found she had nothing to fear, for as Pharaoh's daughter opened the lid and peeked inside the basket, a look of warmth flooded the princess's face. She reached inside and lifted the baby into her arms. He was crying now, his voice becoming louder and louder.

"Why, he must be one of the Hebrew children!" the princess exclaimed. "I think he is hungry."

Suddenly, an idea came to Miriam. Pretending to play along the riverbank, she approached Pharaoh's daughter. "Would you like me to find a Hebrew woman to nurse the baby for you?" she asked.

"Oh yes, and please hurry!" replied the princess.

Miriam ran home as fast as she could go.

"Oh, Mother," young Miriam said as she tried to get her breath. "The Princess . . . Pharaoh's own daughter found the baby."

Jochebed clasped her hands with joy.

"She had a servant bring her the basket," Miriam continued excitedly. "And when she saw the baby, she loved him. All the servants thought he was so cute. I pretended to be playing, but I watched everything that happened."

She told her mother everything that had happened. Then Miriam and Jochebed rushed back to where Pharaoh's daughter held Jochebed's baby in her arms.

"Here, take this child to your home and nurse him for me," the princess instructed Jochebed, "and I will pay you well."

Jochebed and Miriam were overjoyed. They would be able to keep the baby at home under the protection of Pharaoh's daughter, and even more amazing, Jochebed would be paid by the princess to nurse her own son!

"Oh, thank You, God, for saving my baby boy and for giving me such a clever daughter as Miriam," Jochebed prayed joyfully.

So Jochebed nursed her baby, whose name later became Moses, and taught him and his brother, Aaron, and Miriam, all about the wonderful God of Israel who took such good care of them. And ever after, the prophet, Moses, and, indeed, the entire Hebrew nation, were grateful for the quick wits and bravery of young Miriam who had lovingly guarded her baby brother as he lay among the reeds of the Nile River.

Miriam, herself, grew up to become a great Hebrew prophetess and accompanied her brothers, Moses and Aaron, as they led the Hebrew people out of slavery in Egypt to the land promised to them by God.

Hoping in God turns our dark hours into sunshine.

Fear not, for I am with you.
Do not be dismayed. I am your God.
I will strengthen you;
I will help you;
I will uphold you with my
victorious right hand.
ISAIAH 41:10, TLB

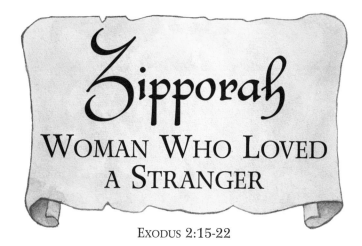

Zipporah
WOMAN WHO LOVED A STRANGER

EXODUS 2:15-22

RE THEY BY THE WELL?" one of the sisters asked.

"Yes, and they won't let us draw water for our sheep," said another.

"Why do they have to be so mean?" cried the youngest.

"Oh come on, we have just as much a right to be here as they do," said Zipporah (ZIP-uh-ruh), the oldest sister, trying to act confident. She grabbed her staff and drove the sheep forward toward the well and its water troughs.

The gang of shepherd youths stared threateningly at the approaching girls. Suddenly, they lunged toward them, yelling and waving their arms to frighten the girls' sheep. They laughed to see the girls scatter and run after the poor frightened sheep.

Then something unexpected happened. A man suddenly rose from the side of the well where he had been resting. He strode toward the shepherd boys and, with one hand, raised two of them off the ground and pitched them into the nearest water trough! The girls laughed and clapped their

hands as the bullies ran away from the well, hurriedly driving their sheep before them.

The stranger bowed to the girls. "I am Moses from the land of Egypt."

The girls gazed at the man in wonder. He was dressed in fine garments, though a bit travel-stained. His hair was cut straight across his forehead in the manner of Egyptians, and he looked as though he might be a nobleman or a prince!

Zipporah was the first to recover her manners. "Good afternoon," she replied, liking the Egyptian at once. "Thank you for coming to our rescue." She introduced herself and her younger sisters to Moses.

Moses helped the girls water their flock of sheep. Then, the girls said goodbye and returned home.

"How did you get the sheep watered so fast today?" their father, Reuel, asked. He was a priest of Midian, the land in which they lived.

"A nice Egyptian man helped us," one daughter told him. "He chased away the shepherd boys, and helped us water the flocks."

"Well, where is he?" their father exclaimed. "Did you just leave him at the well? Go back and invite him to supper!"

The sisters quickly ran back to the well. They were excited. Few strangers came to Midian. It was not a very exciting place—a rocky country fit only for sheep and shepherds.

The Egyptian is so handsome with such good manners, Zipporah thought. *I hope he is still at the well and accepts our dinner invitation.*

Relieved, Zipporah and her sisters found the man in the same place as before. He accepted their invitation gladly and followed them home.

That night, at dinner, Zipporah learned that the man was not really an Egyptian after all. He was a Hebrew by birth, who had been raised in Pharaoh's palace as the adopted son of Pharaoh's daughter!

Zipporah stared dreamily at the man who conversed politely with her father. She had waited all her life for such a man, and she, Zipporah, as eldest daughter of Reuel, had first chance to win his hand in marriage.

Moses . . . Zipporah repeated his name to herself. That's an odd Egyptian name. I wonder how he got it? He is not an ordinary man. What does the future hold for Moses and for the wife of Moses?

Zipporah daydreamed about the man called Moses. She did not know that one day she would marry him, have two sons, and would accompany him to Egypt where he would lead the Hebrews out of Egyptian slavery.

No, Zipporah did not know any of that. All she knew was that she loved this stranger from the desert.

Waiting for the right person to love makes your dreams come true.

For love comes from God and those who are loving and kind show that they are the children of God. . . .
I JOHN 4:7B, TLB

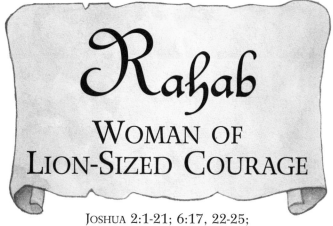

Rahab
WOMAN OF LION-SIZED COURAGE

JOSHUA 2:1-21; 6:17, 22-25;
MATTHEW 1:5; JAMES 2:25

RAHAB (RAY-hab) PUSHED past the two men and ran up the stairs onto the flat roof. "Hurry! Follow me!" she hissed.

Rahab's house was built on top of the thick stone wall surrounding the Amorite city of Jericho. Rahab's house was an inn for travelers. It was also used to manufacture linens and dyes, but that was not all. Rahab's house was also a place of prostitution, for Rahab was a prostitute. A prostitute slept with men for money.

At the moment, however, Rahab was engaged in none of these activities. She was trying to save two men's lives. She motioned for them to hide under one of the piles of flax (blue flowers commonly cultivated and prepared for spinning into cloth) that were stacked and drying on the roof.

In great fear, the men crawled under the flax. They were Hebrew spies sent by Joshua, leader of the Hebrews. They had come to Jericho to discover the best way to attack the city. They had made their way to Rahab's inn hoping to spend the night, but someone had told the king of Jericho about them. At that very moment, soldiers pounded on Rahab's door.

After the men were safely hidden, Rahab raced downstairs to the front door. If she was caught with the spies, she also would be put to death!

"We've heard that there are Hebrew spies in the area," one of the soldiers said. "Have you seen them?"

"The Hebrews were here earlier," she told the officer, "but they left the city at dusk, before the gates closed. Hurry! You might catch them!"

The soldiers ran off toward the city gates. Breathing a sigh of relief, Rahab rushed up the stairs to the roof.

"I know your God is the supreme God of heaven and He will defeat us and give Jericho to your people," Rahab told the Hebrews. "Swear to me, in the name of your God, that when you conquer Jericho, you will let me live, along with everyone in my family."

"We swear that you and your family will not be hurt as long as you stay inside your house during the battle," the men promised Rahab.

Before the men climbed down the scarlet cord she fastened in a window, they told Rahab, "Leave the cord in the window so that our people will know this is your house and they will not destroy it."

The men escaped and told Joshua all that had happened. When they took the city, men were sent to Rahab's house to bring her and her family to safety.

Because of her courage and faith in God, Rahab is listed among the great heroines of the Bible. She became the mother of Boaz who married Ruth, great-grandmother of King David, and took a place in the family line of Jesus.

Strong faith produces strong actions which make heroines.

The godly are bold as lions!
PROVERBS 28:1B, TLB

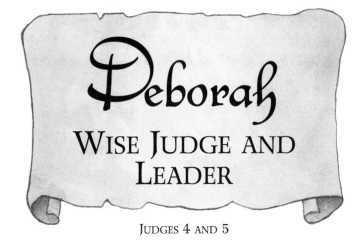

Deborah
WISE JUDGE AND LEADER

JUDGES 4 AND 5

AS A YOUNG GIRL, Deborah had a secret place to go whenever she needed to be by herself. She would sit in the cool shade of a palm tree and think about all that she had heard about the Lord God of Israel. She determined in her heart that she would always follow Him, and Him alone.

There were many troubles in Deborah's life. Her people, the Israelites, were slaves to the Canaanites. The Canaanites were mean and cruel. Their wicked king, Jabin (JAY-bin), and his evil general, Sisera (SISS-uhr-uh), sometimes beat and robbed the Israelites; sometimes they even killed Israelites.

Deborah's own people had turned away from God and had worshiped foreign idols. Many of them no longer prayed to the Lord God. Deborah believed that if only the Israelites would turn back to God, He would help free them from the Canaanites.

God began to speak to Deborah as she sat in the shade of the palm tree. He and Deborah became very close. As Deborah grew older, God told her how to talk about Him to other people and how to help other people solve their problems. It wasn't long before people began to really listen to Deborah.

By the time she was grown, Deborah was well-known as a prophetess of God. She gave the people messages from Him.

Deborah also became a great judge of Israel. The Israelites listened to her wisdom and abided by her decisions. She held her court underneath the shade of the same palm tree that she had visited as a little girl. The palm tree, itself, became famous and was called "Deborah's Palm Tree."

One day, Deborah called a man named Barak (BEAR-uck) to come to her palm tree. "The Lord wants you to lead ten thousand men to Mount Tabor to fight the mighty armies of the Canaanites," she told him. "The Lord says that He will draw the Canaanite army to the Kishon River and will defeat them there."

When he heard those words, Barak became afraid. He knew the Canaanite general, Sisera, had ten times more soldiers than the Israelite army did. Sisera was especially cruel and would bring nine hundred iron chariots into the battle.

"I'll go only if you go with me," Barak told Deborah.

"Okay," Deborah replied, "but the honor of victory will go to a woman instead of to you."

Deborah marched with the soldiers of Israel and led them to the top of Mount Tabor. The Canaanite armies were below at the foot of the mountain by the Kishon River.

"Now is the time to fight!" Deborah told the men. "The Lord will lead you. He has already won the battle for you."

Barak and the men raced down the mountainside to fight the Canaanites. Suddenly, the sky opened up and a fierce hailstorm began to fall down upon the Canaanites. Their eyes were blinded. Their horses stampeded. The entire Canaanite army fell into a panic. Most of them drowned in the river. Some tried to escape into the hills, but Barak's men captured and killed them. The only Canaanite to escape the battle that day was General Sisera. He ran to the tent of Jael, the wife of a man who was a friend of King Jabin. Sisera fell asleep in the tent and was killed by Jael. Just as Deborah had prophesied, the killing of General Sisera and the final victory for Israel was given to a woman!

Deborah and the Israelite soldiers won an important battle against King Jabin and the Canaanites. Under Deborah's continued leadership, and with God's help, Israel grew stronger and stronger until they finally conquered all of the Canaanites. Deborah had brought her nation to victory and back to God.

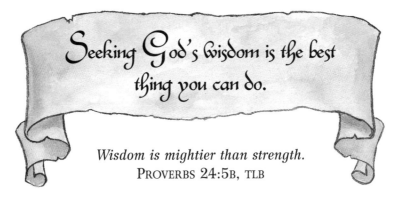

Seeking God's wisdom is the best thing you can do.

Wisdom is mightier than strength.
PROVERBS 24:5B, TLB

Jael

HEROINE OF
ISRAEL

JUDGES 4:17-22; 5:6, 24-27

THE SCREAMS of battle reached Jael's (JAY-els) ears as she hurriedly set down the flask of goat's milk. Now she had something to drink. With fighting so close to her home, she had been afraid to journey to the well for water.

Jael knew what the battle was all about. Her husband, Heber, had told her. The Canaanite king, Jabin, had sent his fiercest general, an evil man named Sisera, to lead the great army to fight the Israelites once and for all. The smaller Israelite army, led by Deborah and Barak, had met Sisera and his army at the Kishon River.

Jael and Heber were Kenites living far away from the rest of their family. Heber had become friends with King Jabin and since Heber was from a family of metal workers, he may have made the iron chariots the king used in battle.

Jael shook her head in wonder. How could her husband be friends with such a king? Jael hated the way King Jabin had made the Israelites his slaves, forcing them to labor in his fields.

Now that the Israelites were fighting the Canaanite army, Jael prayed for their victory, but she did not have much hope. The Canaanite general, Sisera, had ten times more soldiers than the Israelites. Sisera also had nine hundred iron chariots and the Israelites had none.

The battle cries continued. Then, quite suddenly, the sunny sky above Jael's tent turned dark. A mighty storm broke with a torrent of rain and hailstones. Jael watched the storm from the doorway of her tent.

This storm must be from God, Jael told herself. Perhaps it is God's way of helping the Israelite army. Maybe they will win after all!

Before Jael could think any further, a moving object caught her eye. A man was running toward her tent! It was Sisera!

So I was right, Jael thought happily. The Israelites are winning the battle and Sisera is trying to escape from them.

Immediately, a plan came to Jael's mind. She quickly stepped out of her tent and called to Sisera. "Come into my tent! Here, you will be safe under Heber's protection. Don't be afraid."

Sisera went into Jael's tent gladly. He knew that Heber and King Jabin were friends. Surely Sisera would be safe in Heber's tent.

"Please give me some water," Sisera told Jael. "I am very thirsty."

Jael gave Sisera some milk and told him to lie down and rest. She covered him with a blanket.

Sisera was so tired that he soon fell fast asleep. Jael

watched him from the doorway of her tent. She knew God had sent him to her for a purpose. Sisera was an enemy of God and His people. If he were allowed to escape, he would only go back to King Jabin and raise another army. Somehow, Jael must destroy Sisera. But how? She had no weapons.

Glancing around the tent, Jael's eyes rested on a tent peg. It was made of iron and was long with a sharp point at its end. Grabbing it up in her hand, Jael took a hammer and crept quietly alongside Sisera as he slept. With a mighty blow, Jael drove the tent peg through Sisera's head and into the ground.

When Barak, a leader of the Israelite army, came looking for Sisera, Jael took him to her tent and showed him how she had killed the evil general.

Barak was greatly surprised. "Deborah told me in a prophecy that a woman would kill Sisera and win the honor of victory. Today, Jael, you are a heroine of Israel!"

Jael's fame spread throughout Israel. Her name and her deed have never been forgotten.

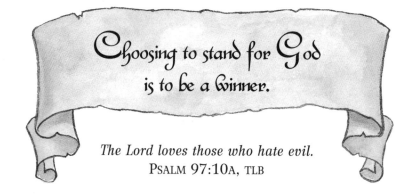

Choosing to stand for God
is to be a winner.

The Lord loves those who hate evil.
PSALM 97:10A, TLB

Woman of Thebez

ONE WHO TOOK AIM FOR GOD

JUDGES 9:50-57

UICK! We'll set the fort of Thebez (THEEBZ) on fire and burn all the people inside!" the evil Abimelech (uh-BIM-uh-leck) called to his men.

Early that morning, Abimelech and his men had destroyed Shechem, killing about a thousand men and women of that city. Now, Abimelech, self-appointed king of Shechem, and his bloodthirsty men planned to do the same to the citizens of the city of Thebez. Those people, too, had fled into a fort that stood inside the city.

"Here they come!" the frightened people cried as Abimelech's men approached. "They are carrying firewood on their shoulders!"

"Oh, no! Abimelech's going to burn us alive just like he burned those others!" the people said as they ran to and fro, weeping in terror.

One woman stood out from all the others. She did not weep or run about, but stared down upon Abimelech and his men with contempt.

"King! Bah!" she hissed out loud. "Nobody wants Abimelech as king. Abimelech has sinned against God. He has set himself up as king of Shechem. He has sinned against his own father, Gideon, who said, "I shall

not be king, nor shall my son be king, the Lord is your King!"

The woman watched as Abimelech piled firewood up against the wall of the fort and, lighting a torch, prepared to set the wood on fire.

"We have to stop him!" the woman cried to the people about her, but no one moved. Looking wildly about her, the woman picked up a heavy millstone. Positioning herself directly over the place where Abimelech stood, the woman hoisted the millstone above her head and, with all her strength, threw it down upon Abimelech's head.

At that instant, Abimelech looked up. He saw the woman above him, but he could not move. The millstone struck his head, splitting his skull.

Crumpling to the ground, Abimelech looked up to see his armor-bearer. "Kill me!" he groaned. "Never let it be said that a woman killed Abimelech."

The young man quickly pierced him with his sword and Abimelech died. When his men saw this, they left and the siege ended.

The people of Thebez praised the woman whose quick action had killed the tyrant and saved them all from burning to death. Even though some would think her weak because she was a woman, God used her to save a city.

Calling on the Lord in weakness makes you strong!

God has chosen the weak things of the world to shame the things which are strong.
I CORINTHIANS 1:27b, NASB

Jephthah's Daughter

VICTOR IN THE TEST OF LOVE

JUDGES 11:30-40

O LORD, if You will help Israel conquer the Ammonites, I will give the first person to come out of my house to meet me as a sacrifice to You!" Jephthah (JEFF-thuh) vowed.

Although he was a cunning warrior, Jephthah had been driven out of his father's house in Gilead by his half brothers. Then, when the Ammonites had attacked Israel, the leaders of Gilead had begged Jephthah to lead their men in battle against the Ammonites. In return, they would make Jephthah chief leader in Gilead.

It is my one chance to become leader and to prove my worth to my brothers, Jephthah told himself.

The need for power caused Jephthah to make such a rash vow to the Lord. He probably thought one of his servants would be the first to meet him upon his return, and he would gladly sacrifice a servant's life for victory in battle.

Jephthah won the battle for Israel. But upon returning home, his daughter ran to meet him, the dearest to his heart.

"Alas, my daughter!" he cried out and fell to the ground. "You have brought me to the dust, for I have made a vow to the Lord and I cannot take

it back." Then he told her of his vow. How he wished he had not made it!

Jephthah's daughter neither cried nor shrank away at her father's words. Courage and faith rang strong in her reply: "Father, you must do whatever you promised the Lord, for He gave you victory in battle. Let me go up into the hills with my girlfriends for two months and weep because now I'll never marry and never have children of my own."

Yes," Jephthah replied sadly, noting that she would spend her last days with others rather than with him. Jephthah's heart was broken.

Jephthath's daughter went to the hills and there found the strength needed to face what lay ahead. She did not run away, as many others might have done. Instead, she returned and gave her own life to fulfill her father's vow. In so doing, she became the real victor, showing her father what real love is all about—putting others' needs before our own.

Though Jephthath won an earthly battle and received the glory of being a leader, his daughter won much more. Because her sacrifice was not for her own gain, but for someone else, her sacrifice was greater.

The people of Israel did not forget Jephthah's daughter. It became a custom in Israel for young girls to leave their homes for four days each year to remember the heroic deed that Jephthah's daughter did that day.

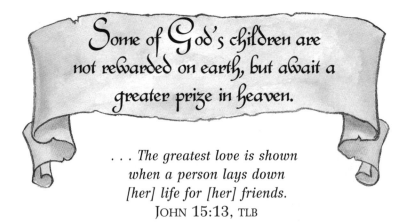

Some of God's children are not rewarded on earth, but await a greater prize in heaven.

. . . *The greatest love is shown*
when a person lays down
[her] life for [her] friends.
JOHN 15:13, TLB

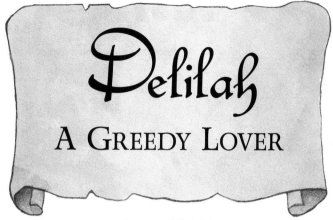

Delilah

A GREEDY LOVER

JUDGES 16:4-31

HE FIVE PHILISTINE (fih-LISS-teen) LEADERS stared down at Delilah (deh-LIE-lah). "Find out what makes Samson so strong so we can capture him and we will give you five thousand dollars for the information."

"Okay," Delilah agreed. She would go along with the leaders so she could get rich with their money!

Delilah remembered the stories about Samson's mighty strength. He had killed thirty men to pay off a bet, and he had tied a fiery torch onto the tails of three hundred foxes and let them run through Philistine fields, burning the harvest to the ground. All of these things Samson had done to get back at his enemies, the Philistines. Now they wanted to take him prisoner.

"Samson delights in cruelty and killing," Delilah told herself. "He sleeps with prostitutes whenever he can. He says he loves me but I don't think Samson knows the meaning of love. He may be strong, but he is weak in spirit. It will not be too hard to find out his secret!"

That night when Samson came to visit Delilah, she begged, "Please tell me, Samson, why you are so strong."

"Well," Samson replied, "if I were tied with seven leather bowstrings, I would become as weak as anyone else."

After he fell asleep, Delilah tied him with seven bowstrings. Then she yelled, "Samson! The Philistines are here!"

Samson awoke and snapped the bowstrings as if they were thread.

"Samson," Delilah pouted, "you did not tell the truth. Now tell me how you can be captured!"

"If I am tied with brand-new ropes, I will be as weak as other men."

Again Samson fell asleep and Delilah used new ropes to tie him up.

"Samson! The Philistines have come to capture you!" Delilah cried, but Samson awoke and broke the ropes as if they were spiderwebs.

"You told another lie," Delilah frowned. "How can you be captured?"

"If you weave my hair into a loom, I will be as weak as other men."

While Samson slept, Delilah wove his hair into a loom and cried, "The Philistines have come!" He awoke and yanked his hair from the loom.

"How can you say you love me when you don't tell me the truth?" Delilah whined. She used her charms upon him until finally he told her his secret.

"My hair has never been cut. I was born a Nazirite, a special servant of God. If my hair is cut, I will become as weak as anyone else."

Delilah knew Samson had told the truth. She called the Philistine leaders who came to her with their money. Delilah lulled Samson to sleep with his head in her lap. Then a barber came and cut off Samson's hair.

"The Philistines are here to capture you, Samson!" Delilah screamed as she shook Samson.

Samson awoke but could do nothing. His strength was gone. The Philistines captured him and put him in prison. He was blinded and made to work hard grinding at a mill.

Then one day at the temple, something amazing happened. As the Philistine people celebrated the capture of Samson, soldiers brought him out and made him stand between two pillars at the center of the temple. The

Philistines called out Samson's name and laughed at him. Delilah watched from the grandstand as Samson was mocked. He stood with bowed head, as if in prayer, then suddenly, he took hold of the pillars and pushed. The temple crashed down upon Samson, Delilah, and all the people.

Refusing to participate in evil schemes, no matter what the payoff, can save your life.

What profit is there if you gain the whole world—and lose eternal life?
MATTHEW 16:26A, TLB

Orpah

FAIR-WEATHER
FRIEND

RUTH 1:1-14

RPAH (OR-puh) STARED at the backs of the two women that marched in front of her. One back was old and bent under the strain of too many sorrows; yet it went at a steady pace challenging Orpah to keep up. The second back was young and strong; determined to continue on.

"Right! Left! Right! Left! Keep moving! Keep moving! To Bethlehem! To Bethlehem! Right! Left!" the backs seemed to say.

Orpah sighed and looked down at her dust-covered feet, the bottom hem of her blue traveling robe already a dirt-brown color. Did this road stretch on forever? Would her mother-in-law, Naomi, ever stop? Did her sister-in-law, Ruth, ever want to rest?

Orpah tried to think of something pleasant, but it was impossible. Too many bad things had happened. Naomi's son, Chilion (KILL-ih-uhn) had married Orpah, and her other son, Mahlon (MAH-luhn), had married Ruth. Both had recently died. Naomi's own husband, Elimelech, had died several years ago. Now all three women were widows. There were no men left in the family.

Naomi is going back to her hometown of Bethlehem, but I don't really want to go, thought Orpah. *The Jews of Bethlehem don't like foreigners. Ruth and I are Moabites. We'll never have any friends or find anyone to marry. We'll be stuck in the house of Naomi forever, and she has turned old and bitter and is no fun to be with!*

As if reading Orpah's thoughts, Naomi suddenly stopped smack in the center of the road. "Why don't you girls return to your parents' homes in Moab instead of coming with me to Bethlehem?" she suggested. "Perhaps you will each find another husband and you will have happy homes again."

Orpah protested feebly, but after further urging from Naomi, kissed her mother-in-law goodbye and turned back down the road, this time heading for her own childhood home in Moab. Orpah's feet no longer felt tired. She would run home! She was free again!

Orpah stopped suddenly. She had forgotten to wait for Ruth! Turning around, Orpah did not see Ruth following along behind her. Where was she?

Squinting into the distance, Orpah could barely see two small figures, their backs moving in a familiar rhythm. Left! Right!

"Ruth is going with Naomi to Bethlehem!" she gasped. For a moment, she wavered. Should she, like Ruth, be faithful and remain with Naomi?

"But I'm tired of feeling sad," Orpah told herself. "I want to be happy and carefree again."

Orpah turned away once more. This time, she did not look back. She ran quickly to her Moabite home and did not think again of Naomi and Ruth.

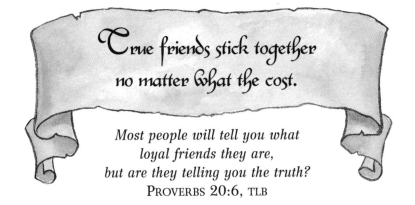

True friends stick together
no matter what the cost.

*Most people will tell you what
loyal friends they are,
but are they telling you the truth?*
PROVERBS 20:6, TLB

Naomi

BITTER WOMAN
MADE GLAD

RUTH 1:1-18

"GOOD-BYE, ORPAH!" Naomi called. With a heavy heart, she watched the younger woman walk away and turn south to hurry back down the earthen road that ran through the land of Moab. Her shawl was tightly wound about her head and neck, a protection against heat and dust.

Naomi sighed. She would never see Orpah again. They had once been a family—a big, happy family. Naomi's son, Mahlon, had married Ruth and her other son, Chilion, had married Orpah. They had all lived together, Naomi's own husband having died years ago.

Naomi had been so thankful for her two daughters-in-law, Ruth and Orpah. They had spent many glad hours talking and laughing, as they baked bread or worked in the garden. Even though Ruth and Orpah were not Hebrews, they had been eager to learn the Hebrew customs. They had even begun to learn about the Lord God of Israel, whom the Hebrews worshiped.

Now the happy times are all gone, Naomi told herself. Quite suddenly, both Mahlon and Chilion had died, and Naomi, Ruth, and Orpah were left alone. Naomi had decided to leave the land of Moab and return to her hometown of Bethlehem with her two daughters-in-law, but after starting upon the journey, Naomi had changed her mind. She told Ruth and Orpah to return to their parents' homes in Moab where the young women would have more of a chance to start over and lead normal, happy lives.

Orpah had agreed to Naomi's suggestion and had left to go back to her Moabite home. Ruth, however, would not leave Naomi. She insisted upon going with Naomi even though she had been warned that she would not be accepted by the Bethlehem Hebrews and there would have no chance to marry.

Tears came to Naomi's eyes as she heard Ruth promise never to leave her. Instead of returning home, Ruth committed to caring for Naomi.

Naomi had never witnessed such loyalty. How could a young woman like Ruth be willing to sacrifice her life to remain with an old woman like Naomi? Within her sad and bitter heart, Naomi felt a prick of light, a tenderness for the young Moabite woman who refused to abandon her. The love Ruth showed to Naomi made the sadness a little easier to bear.

I am not alone for I have Ruth, Naomi told herself. Together, we will travel to Bethlehem and see what the Lord has in store for us.

With that thought, Naomi turned her back on Orpah, tightened her own shawl around her, and with Ruth by her side, began the long journey back to Bethlehem.

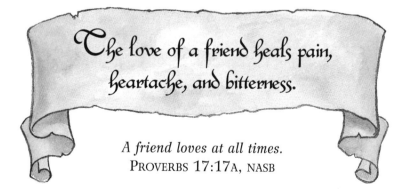

The love of a friend heals pain, heartache, and bitterness.

A friend loves at all times.
PROVERBS 17:17A, NASB

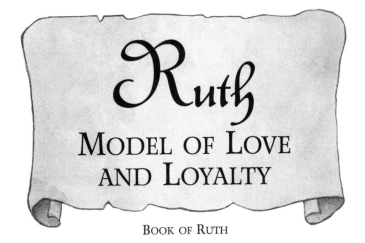

Ruth

MODEL OF LOVE AND LOYALTY

BOOK OF RUTH

WE HAVE ONLY BEEN WALKING *a short while and already my poor mother-in-law looks tired,* Ruth thought to herself. *I hope Naomi can make it all the way to Bethlehem.*

Ruth and her sister-in-law, Orpah, were traveling with Naomi. They were poor and had no money to buy camels to ride. They had to walk.

Many sad things had happened. First, Naomi's husband, Elimelech, had died; then some years later, both of Naomi's sons, Chilion and Mahlon, died. Chilion had married Orpah, and Mahlon had married Ruth. Now the three women—Naomi, Ruth, and Orpah—were left alone without their husbands. Without food or money, a husband or sons, Naomi felt sad and empty inside. She decided to return to Bethlehem, her homeland.

Naomi stopped suddenly in the road. "You girls shouldn't come with me to Israel," she told Ruth and Orpah. "You should go back to your parents' homes in Moab. Then you will have a chance to marry again and have happy lives."

"Oh, no," Ruth and Orpah cried together. "We want to go with you."

But Naomi replied, "No, you should return to your own people. You should not be stuck with me. I am too old and do not have any other sons for you to marry."

The young women and Naomi cried together. Orpah kissed Naomi good-bye and returned to her childhood home, but Ruth would not leave Naomi. She loved her mother-in-law very much. Even though it was scary to leave her homeland, Ruth was determined to stay with Naomi.

"Do not ask me to leave you," Ruth told Naomi, "for wherever you go, I will go, and wherever you live, I will live. Your people shall be my people, and your God shall be my God. Where you die, I will die, and there I will be buried. May God do terrible things to me if I allow anything to separate us!"

Naomi stared in surprise at her young daughter-in-law. Never had she witnessed such determined love and loyalty.

"You mean you would give up all of your chances for a happy life in your own country just for me?" Naomi whispered. "May God bless you for it!"

Ruth and Naomi journeyed onward. They did not stop until they reached the small city of Bethlehem in Israel.

Life in Bethlehem was not easy. Ruth and Naomi were still very poor. One day, Ruth went to a field where men were reaping barley. Ruth walked behind the men and gathered up all the grain that the men did not glean. She put it in her basket and saved it to make flour for bread.

"Who is that woman?" Boaz asked the men. Boaz was the owner of the field.

"That's the Moabite woman who came back with Naomi," the foreman of the reapers told him.

Boaz went over to talk to Ruth. "Stay in my field and you will be safe. You may drink my water when you're thirsty. Come and eat lunch with us."

"Thank you, sir," Ruth replied. "Why are you so kind to me? I am only a foreigner."

"I have heard all about the love you have shown to Naomi and how you left your own family to come and live with her here among strangers. May God bless you for it!"

Boaz gave Ruth extra barley. She also gathered wheat from his fields. Soon she and Boaz were married. Ruth had a baby son. Naomi was so happy to have a little grandson.

"You have a little boy again," the women of the city told Naomi. "Your daughter-in-law, Ruth, has done more for you than seven sons!"

Ruth's son was named Obed. He later became the grandfather of King David, an ancestor of Jesus. In this way, Ruth, a Gentile from Moab, became part of the family line of Jesus. God did indeed bless her for the loyalty she had shown to Naomi!

Sacrificing your life for another
is to be like Jesus.

If you love someone you will be loyal to [her] no matter what the cost.
I CORINTHIANS 13:7A, TLB

Hannah
WOMAN WHO KEPT HER PROMISE

I SAMUEL 1—2:11, 19-21

COVERING HER HEAD WITH A SHAWL, Hannah slipped into the evening shadows and made her way through the paths of Shiloh to the tabernacle. She was deeply distressed.

Oh, if only I had a child, she thought. *I would be so happy.* As the first wife of Elkanah (el-KAY-nuh), she had been unable to have children. Elkanah's second wife, Peninnah (puh-NIN-uh), had many children and constantly made fun of Hannah for having none.

Every year, the family journeyed to the tabernacle to sacrifice to the Lord. Elkanah would give Peninnah and her children many presents, but he could give Hannah only one present because she had no children.

Reaching the tabernacle, Hannah made a vow to the Lord: "Oh Lord, if You will give me a son, I will give him back to You for his entire lifetime."

Eli, the priest of the tabernacle, noticed Hannah's mouth moving but heard no sound (she prayed silently to herself). He thought she was drunk!

"Must you come here drunk?" Eli demanded.

"Oh, no, sir, I was only pouring my heart out to the Lord," Hannah replied quickly. "Please don't think I am a drunk."

81

"May the Lord grant you your request," Eli replied after a moment.

Hannah returned home to the hill country of Ramah. God remembered Hannah's prayer and soon she became pregnant! When her baby boy was born, she named him *Samuel* which means "asked of God."

That year, Hannah did not go to the tabernacle. "I will stay home with Samuel until he is weaned from my milk. Then I will take him to the tabernacle. I must keep my promise to the Lord," Hannah said to Elkanah.

"Whatever you think best," replied Elkanah.

After Samuel was weaned and even though he was still small, Hannah and Elkanah took him to the tabernacle and presented him to Eli.

"Remember me?" Hannah asked Eli. "I prayed to the Lord and asked Him for this child and now I am giving him to God for as long as he lives."

So Hannah kept her promise to God and left Samuel at the tabernacle. Each year she brought him a new little coat to wear. God rewarded Hannah by giving her five more children—two daughters and three sons!

Although Samuel was not born into the priesthood as most Hebrew priests, he was sacredly pledged to the Lord by his mother. She passed her faith on to Samuel and even though the family of Eli was soon discovered to be wicked, Samuel remained true to the Lord. As a man, he became a great prophet and judge of Israel, counseling King Saul and King David.

Only God can measure the true value of a mother. Had it not been for Hannah's prayer and promise to the Lord, Israel would have had no Samuel.

Crying out to the Lord brings help!

Because he [the Lord] bends down and listens, I will pray as long as I breathe!
PSALM 116:2, TLB

Michal

PRINCESS WITH COURAGE

I Samuel 18:20-30; 19:9-17

"IF YOU DON'T GET AWAY TONIGHT, you'll be dead by morning," Michal (MY-hull) warned her husband, David. "My father and his soldiers will kill you!"

It was true. King Saul was so jealous of David that he had tried several times to kill him, even though his daughter, Michal, and her brother, Jonathan, had pleaded for David's life.

"Why would you kill my husband?" Michal asked her father.

"Don't you remember how David killed Goliath and brought you a great victory?" Jonathan asked King Saul.

But it was no use. Because of his victories in battle, David had become more popular than King Saul and the king was furious. Why just now Saul had thrown a spear at David while David had played a harp for the king's enjoyment!

"Help me to get away!" David cried to Michal. He was gathering together his bow, arrows, knife, and water skin, and pulling on his travel cloak.

"There are soldiers across the road waiting for you to come out the door," Michal told David as she peeked out a front window.

"I'll go out a back window," David decided.

Michal helped David to climb out the window. She watched anxiously as he crawled away in the darkness. Would she ever see him again? The king's soldiers were everywhere. What could she do to stall the soldiers and give David more time to escape?

Running to the bedroom, Michal took a large idol and put it into the bed. She covered it with blankets and put its head on a pillow of goat hair. If the soldiers didn't look too closely, they might think that it was David lying in the bed.

Nervous and afraid, Michal stayed awake all night. She hated going against her father, but she had to protect David. She loved David, and she knew he was favored by the Lord.

"Lord, please help him," she prayed, "and make my plan to trick the soldiers work tomorrow."

In the morning, the soldiers came to arrest David. Michal told them that he was sick and couldn't get out of bed. One of the officers entered the house and peeked into the bedroom. When he saw the lump under the covers and the goat hair on the pillow, he believed David was really in bed.

The soldiers left, but soon came back again. "The king has ordered me to bring your husband in his bed!" an officer told Michal. The soldiers entered the bedroom to carry out David and the bed, but they immediately discovered Michal's trick! Angrily, they took her to King Saul.

"Why have you deceived me and let my enemy escape?" the king demanded of his daughter. His face was twisted with fury. He had allowed jealousy and anger to rage within him until he thought of nothing but his hatred for David. He would kill his own children to capture David. Michal knew she had better think of something to ease her father's anger or she would soon die herself!

"I had to help him," she pleaded. "He threatened to kill me, Father, if I didn't help him."

King Saul stared at her angrily, then turned away.

Michal left her father's presence, not daring to let out her breath until she had rounded several corners in the palace.

"Thank You, Lord," she finally gasped. She had done all she could. Now, David's life was in the hands of the Lord.

Have courage to take the
risk for what is right.

*Be strong, and let your heart
take courage. . . .*
PSALM 27:14B, NASB

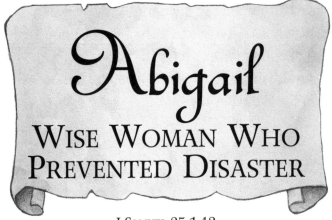

Abigail
WISE WOMAN WHO PREVENTED DISASTER

I SAMUEL 25:1-42

H, HELP US! Do something quick! David and his men are coming to kill us all!" the frightened young man cried out to Abigail.

"Calm down and explain yourself," Abigail replied.

"It all started this morning," he told her. "David sent some men to Nabal to ask him for food. David and his men live in the wilderness because King Saul is chasing after them. Now they have run out of food. But when they asked Nabal for help, he insulted them. David and his men are very angry and are riding here to kill us!" The young man looked pleadingly at Abigail. "You are Nabal's wife. Only you can save us!"

Abigail heard the young man with dismay. *My mean husband has done it again,* she thought. *Time after time, Nabal angers people with his stubborn, ill-mannered ways. Always it is up to me to make amends!*

Wasting no time, Abigail called the servants to help pack food onto donkeys. They packed two hundred loaves of bread, two barrels of wine, five slain sheep, two bushels of grain, one hundred raisin cakes, and two hundred fig cakes. They packed all of this without Nabal knowing about it.

Telling the young man to ride ahead, Abigail followed with the donkeys laden with food. Soon they met David and his men riding toward their ranch. Abigail quickly dismounted and bowed low before David. She knew she had to act quickly.

"I accept all blame in this matter, my lord," Abigail addressed David. "I did not see the messengers you sent to my husband, Nabal. Please accept these presents from me. Pay no attention to Nabal. He is known for the bad decisions he makes. I pray that all your enemies shall be cursed like Nabal. The Lord will surely reward you for fighting His battles, but when you are King of Israel, you won't want the murder of Nabal on your conscience. God will bring you success, and when He does, please remember me!"

A moment of surprised silence passed as David stared into the wise eyes of Abigail. Then his face relaxed and a smile replaced his frown.

"Bless the Lord for sending you to meet me today! I thank God for your good sense!" David exclaimed. "You have kept me from murdering Nabal and all of his men and taking vengeance into my own hands."

David accepted Abigail's gifts and told her to return home without fear. He would not attack them.

At home, Nabal had thrown a big party and was very drunk. *I'll tell him about my meeting with David tomorrow*, Abigail thought.

The next morning, she asked God, "Please help me tell Nabal about my meeting with David. Protect me from his terrible anger."

Relying on God's protection, Abigail talked to Nabal, but as soon as he heard her news, Nabal suffered a stroke and fell paralyzed at her feet! The servants put him in bed where he lay for ten days and then died.

"The Lord has dealt with Nabal," Abigail told her friends. "It was God's way of releasing me from my marriage."

When news of Nabal's death reached David, he said, "Praise God! He has wreaked His own vengeance on Nabal and, through Abigail, kept me from doing it myself."

David sent messages to Abigail to ask her to become his wife. She eagerly agreed. Although David was not yet king, Abigail believed God's promise to make David king someday. She rode from her house to marry David, and he was ever grateful for her wisdom that had prevented him from murdering Nabal and his household.

Kind words win arguments and are a mark of godly wisdom and self-control.

A soft answer turns away wrath, but harsh words cause quarrels.
PROVERBS 15:1, TLB

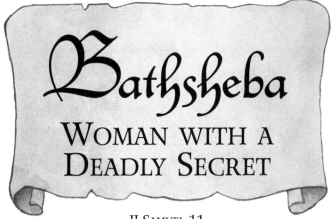

Bathsheba

WOMAN WITH A DEADLY SECRET

II SAMUEL 11

HY HAS THE KING SENT FOR ME? Bathsheba wondered, hurrying after the king's messenger. *King David has never asked me to the palace before!*

Reaching the palace, Bathsheba bowed low before King David and waited for him to speak.

"The other night, I noticed you taking a bath on the roof of your house," David said to Bathsheba. "You are very beautiful."

Bathsheba looked into the king's eyes and knew instantly what he wanted. An uncomfortable feeling swept over her. She was a married woman and she had never been unfaithful to her husband. Now she knew that David wanted her to break the vow that she had made to her husband, Uriah. It was wrong but what could she do? He was the king! She had been told all of her life to obey the king's orders. Besides, it was supposed to be an honor if the king desired you.

So King David slept with Bathsheba and a little later, Bathsheba found that she was pregnant.

"Now what do I do?" Bathsheba worried. "Uriah, who has been away for

91

Bathsheba

WOMAN WITH A DEADLY SECRET

II SAMUEL 11

HY HAS THE KING SENT FOR ME? Bathsheba wondered, hurrying after the king's messenger. *King David has never asked me to the palace before!*

Reaching the palace, Bathsheba bowed low before King David and waited for him to speak.

"The other night, I noticed you taking a bath on the roof of your house," David said to Bathsheba. "You are very beautiful."

Bathsheba looked into the king's eyes and knew instantly what he wanted. An uncomfortable feeling swept over her. She was a married woman and she had never been unfaithful to her husband. Now she knew that David wanted her to break the vow that she had made to her husband, Uriah. It was wrong but what could she do? He was the king! She had been told all of her life to obey the king's orders. Besides, it was supposed to be an honor if the king desired you.

So King David slept with Bathsheba and a little later, Bathsheba found that she was pregnant.

"Now what do I do?" Bathsheba worried. "Uriah, who has been away for

Bathsheba

WOMAN WITH A DEADLY SECRET

II SAMUEL 11

HY HAS THE KING SENT FOR ME? Bathsheba wondered, hurrying after the king's messenger. *King David has never asked me to the palace before!*

Reaching the palace, Bathsheba bowed low before King David and waited for him to speak.

"The other night, I noticed you taking a bath on the roof of your house," David said to Bathsheba. "You are very beautiful."

Bathsheba looked into the king's eyes and knew instantly what he wanted. An uncomfortable feeling swept over her. She was a married woman and she had never been unfaithful to her husband. Now she knew that David wanted her to break the vow that she had made to her husband, Uriah. It was wrong but what could she do? He was the king! She had been told all of her life to obey the king's orders. Besides, it was supposed to be an honor if the king desired you.

So King David slept with Bathsheba and a little later, Bathsheba found that she was pregnant.

"Now what do I do?" Bathsheba worried. "Uriah, who has been away for

several weeks fighting in the king's army, will surely know I have become pregnant by another man. Legally, he could have me killed for committing adultery!"

In desperation, Bathsheba sent a note to King David informing him of her condition. The king immediately asked that Uriah be sent to him from battle. After chatting with him awhile, David sent Uriah home to spend the night with Bathsheba. That way, the king hoped Uriah would believe that he had been the one to make Bathsheba pregnant. But Uriah did not go home. He slept in the palace gateway with the other servants of the king.

"Why didn't you go home?" David asked him the next morning.

"I would have felt guilty sleeping with my wife when the other soldiers are camping out in open fields," Uriah explained.

The next night, David again tried to convince Uriah to go home to his wife, but he refused. Finally, David sent Uriah back to the battle with a note to his commanding officer ordering him to put Uriah in the front lines of battle where he would surely be killed.

Uriah was killed and Bathsheba mourned for him, but when the mourning period was over, David made Bathsheba one of his wives and she gave birth to his son.

God was displeased with David's actions and sent Nathan, a prophet, to tell the king that he had sinned.

"Because of your sin, murder will be a constant threat in your house," Nathan warned David. "Your family will rebel against you. Your wives will be given to another man. You will not die from this sin, but your baby will."

When Bathsheba heard of the prophet's words, she grew terribly afraid. Her baby became very ill and she prayed constantly for the baby to live. David went without food and lay on the bare earth praying to God, asking God to forgive his wrongdoing and let the baby live. But the baby died.

The death of her baby and experiencing firsthand the effects of sin must have had a profound effect on Bathsheba. David continued to battle, kill, and enslave other people. His sons (from other wives) murdered each other, raped their sister, and rebelled against David. Bathsheba, however, mothered four sons and devoted herself to them. Perhaps she read them psalms that their father had written as a young shepherd. Her most famous son, Solomon, became king after David's death. Testifying to his mother's godly training, he wrote Proverbs 22:6 that states: "Teach a child to choose the right path, and when he is older he will remain upon it." (TLB)

What Bathsheba did with the rest of her life, we do not know. But God will someday reveal and reward all that we have done, whether good or bad.

God will help you out of every situation if you choose to follow His ways.

I will trust and not be afraid,
for the Lord is my strength
and song; he is my salvation.
ISAIAH 12:2B, TLB

Tamar, David's Daughter

BEAUTIFUL VICTIM OF SIN

II SAMUEL 13:1-30

AMAR HURRIED to the house of her half brother, Amnon. He was sick, and her father, King David, had asked her to cook for Amnon because he liked her company. Tamar, known for her cooking abilities, was also very beautiful, and a favorite among her brothers.

"Come and bake me some bread," Amnon told Tamar as soon as she entered his room. "You see, I am sick."

Tamar went into Amnon's bedroom so he could watch her mix up the dough. But when the bread was ready, he refused to eat it!

"Everyone, get out of here!" Amnon suddenly ordered the servants.

After they had left, he said to Tamar, "Feed me the bread!"

Tamar took him the bread, but as she stood before him, he grabbed her and demanded, "Come to bed with me!"

"Amnon, please don't do this to me!" she cried as she struggled to free herself from his grip. "I would be so ashamed. If you love me, ask the king and he will let you marry me."

But Amnon wouldn't listen to her and because he was stronger, he forced her to go to bed with him. Then, afterward, he hated her.

95

"Get out of here!" Amnon snarled at Tamar.

"Oh, no!" Tamar pleaded. "For it is an even greater sin to reject me after what you did to me."

But again, he would not listen to her. He called his servant to throw Tamar out of his room.

Crying, Tamar ran away. She tore her robe and put ashes on her head. Her brother, Absalom, asked her, "Is it true that Amnon raped you?"

Tamar nodded. She was so upset, she could not speak.

"Don't worry," Absalom told her. "Let's keep the news of this in our family alone. You can live with me in my house."

Sadly, Tamar went to live in disgrace in Absalom's house. King David was furious when he heard the news, but he did not punish Amnon for his crime. But Absalom hated Amnon for what he had done to Tamar. Two years later, at a family feast, Absalom had Amnon killed. Afterward, Absalom fled from his father, King David.

Eventually, Absalom returned. He had three sons and a beautiful little daughter whom he named Tamar. But sin ran deep in David's house. Absalom tried to take the kingship away from David and was killed.

What became of Tamar was never recorded. By now, she is in the arms of her heavenly Father. He has healed Tamar's hurts and has dried Tamar's tears just as He promises to do with all of His children.

God is a Father who loves you perfectly.

The Lord replies, "I will arise and defend the oppressed, the poor, the needy. I will rescue them as they have longed for me to do."
PSALM 12:5, TLB

Wise Woman of Abel
One Who Turned Away an Army

II Samuel 20:16-22

 LOSE THE CITY GATES! Quick! King David's soldiers are preparing to attack the city of Abel!" a man cried loudly.

"How can that be?" asked a woman, but the man did not answer. The woman, an influential citizen of Abel, ran to the city gates just as they banged shut. Finding the gates barred, the woman climbed up to the top of the outer wall and looked over. Soldiers just below her were busily building a mound to the top of the city wall in order to batter it down.

"What madness is this?" the woman cried out loudly.

The soldiers paused in their activity to look at her in surprise. Why was a woman standing on top of the wall directly in their line of attack?

The woman paid no attention to the soldiers. Spotting their general, she called, "Joab! Listen to me! Come over here so I can talk to you!"

Too surprised to refuse, the commander in chief of David's army approached the woman.

"It is said that if you want to settle an argument, ask advice at Abel, because we always give wise counsel," the woman told Joab. "Why are you

98

destroying an ancient, peace-loving city that is loyal to Israel?"

"We are not here to destroy the city," Joab told her. "We only want a traitor named Sheba who has revolted against King David. He has taken refuge in your city. Give him to me and we will leave the city in peace."

"All right," the woman replied, "we will throw his head over the wall to you."

Going back to her people, the woman spoke to the leaders of the city, "It is better to kill Sheba, a rebel and a traitor, than to get into a fight with the king's soldiers," the woman advised. "The soldiers are stronger than we are and could easily overrun our city. Many innocent people might be killed before they found Sheba. Let us give Joab the head of this bad man, and he and his army will leave."

Believing this to be wise advice, the people of Abel killed Sheba and threw his head out to Joab. A trumpet was blown and the soldiers were called back from their attack. By one woman's quick wit and courage, the city of Abel was saved and the rebel Sheba was destroyed, securing peace in the kingdom of David.

It is better to settle an argument quickly than to use force and angry words.

Ability to give wise advice satisfies like a good meal!
PROVERBS 18:20, TLB

Rizpah

MOTHER WHOSE LOVE WAS STRONGER THAN DEATH

II Samuel 3:7; 21:1-14

AKE THE FIVE SONS OF MERAB (ME-rab), Saul's daughter, and the two sons of Rizpah (RIZZ-puh), Saul's concubine, and hang them before the Lord," King David told the Gibeonite leaders. "Then perhaps the guilt of Saul's deeds against your country will be washed from Israel and the famine will end."

"Oh, no!" Rizpah screamed as David's men handed over her two sons, Armoni and Mephibosheth (muh-FIB-uh-sheth), to the angry soldiers of Gibeon. "Don't take my sons," she sobbed.

They were chained together with the five sons of Merab and made to march with the Gibeonite soldiers to a mountainside. Rizpah followed behind them, grieving as only a mother can grieve for her children.

As a young girl, Rizpah had been taken to the palace to be one of King Saul's concubines. She had been given no choice. Females were bought and sold as possessions at that time. Rizpah had become pregnant by Saul and had given him two sons. Because Saul had tried to destroy their country, the Gibeonites wanted to kill Rizpah's sons as payment for their father's sins.

As soon as they reached the mountainside, the soldiers killed the seven young men. They hung their bodies from trees upon a hilltop near the city of Gibeon, so that all could see that Saul's crimes against them were now paid.

Rizpah tore her clothing and tore out her hair. Her sons had been her only family and the only ones who had truly loved her. She had cared for them in life. Now she would care for them in death.

Spreading sackcloth upon a rock, Rizpah stayed beside the bodies of her two sons as they hung from a tree. For an entire harvest season, she guarded them from the vultures and wild animals. She had no shelter, and no food or water. Yet she did not leave them. As long as she had breath in her body, she would protect the bodies of her sons.

The people of Gibeon were amazed at Rizpah's commitment to her sons. Never before had anyone displayed such devotion. News of Rizpah finally reached King David. He sent men to take down the bodies of the young men and to bury them with the bones of their father, Saul.

Rizpah's long vigil was over. Her sons' bodies were safe. She could take comfort in the knowledge that one day, men's crimes will be judged by the one God who does not forget the cries of mothers and children. He will defend the innocent as passionately as Rizpah defended her own sons' lifeless bodies, and He will bring their tormentors to justice.

God withheld the rain until Rizpah's sons were buried; then He sent it to fall upon the land to end the famine.

Shine with God's love and passionately defend the weak and innocent.

For the needs of the needy shall not be ignored forever, the hopes of the poor shall not always be crushed.
PSALM 9:18, TLB

Queen of Sheba

LOVER OF KNOWLEDGE AND WISDOM

II CHRONICLES 9:1-12;
MATTHEW 12:42

AMELS PARADED in a long line through the streets of Jerusalem. They carried heavy bundles of gold, spices, and jewels for King Solomon. The gold alone measured 120 talents, worth about $3,500,000! The camels followed after a rich and ornate travel coach that stopped outside the steps of the king's palace.

"Ohhhhhhh," the people said to one another. "A very important person has come to visit the king."

Stepping from the coach was the most beautifully adorned queen the city had ever seen. She was the Queen of Sheba, known not only for her beauty, but also for her keen mind and probing intellect. Traveling nearly 1,200 miles, she had come to see if the stories concerning Solomon's wisdom were true.

Though the queen possessed great wealth and riches, she valued wisdom more. She was a seeker of knowledge and came with hard questions to test Solomon's wisdom.

"I've heard that Solomon's great wisdom comes from the Lord God of Israel," she said as she climbed the stairs. "I want to hear more about this

God." Her servants looked at each other. They knew that the queen would not be satisfied until she got the answers she was looking for.

King Solomon met the queen and they spent many hours talking. God opened Solomon's mind so that the king could answer all of the queen's questions. Nothing was left hidden. Everything was answered! How God must have loved this queen who journeyed so far to find out more truth about Him!

Indeed, when Jesus came into the world, He told the crowds that the queen of the south (the Queen of Sheba) would rise up and condemn them because she had journeyed far to hear the wisdom of Solomon. Yet many of Jesus' hearers did not even recognize that Jesus as Lord was greater than Solomon!

"Everything I heard about you is true," she said to Solomon as she boarded her coach. "Your wisdom is far greater than I imagined. Blessed be the Lord your God!"

The queen and the king exchanged rare and beautiful presents worth millions of dollars. But the queen took back to her people a far greater gift—knowledge about the Lord God!

Put the wisdom of God ahead of wealth and beauty and you, too, will be wise.

Knowing God results in
every other kind of understanding.
PROVERBS 9:10B, TLB

Jezebel
QUEEN WHO LOVED EVIL

I Kings 16—19; 21; 22;
II Kings 1; 8—10; 13—14; 25-28

EZEBEL HAD GROWN UP worshiping idols. She particularly worshiped the false god Baal. And as she grew older, she married the wicked king from Israel named Ahab. The king was also a worshiper of Baal; he built a magnificent temple in Samaria for Baal. Soon many of the Israelites worshiped Baal. They turned their hearts away from the one true God.

This made God very angry. God sent Elijah, the prophet, to give King Ahab this message: "As surely as the Lord God of Israel lives, there won't be any dew or rain for several years until I say the word!"

No rain fell on the land for three years. Then Elijah called for a contest on Mount Carmel between the false god and the one true God. The people would see who would send fire to burn up the sacrifices that had been placed on each altar there.

Four hundred and fifty prophets of Baal and four hundred prophets of Asherah danced about their altar for several hours, asking their god to light the wood, but nothing happened. They did many things to get the attention of their god, but to no avail.

"Maybe your god is sleeping," Elijah called out to the prophets.

When it was Elijah's turn, he simply prayed to the Lord God and fire was sent to burn the sacrifice!

"Now we know who the true God is," many people said. "We will worship the Lord God of Israel." All of the prophets of Baal and Asherah were killed. Then the heavens opened up and rain fell on the earth. When Queen Jezebel heard what had happened, she was furious. How dare a prophet of God kill her prophets! She sent a message to Elijah that said: "You killed my prophets and now I swear by the gods that I am going to kill you by this time tomorrow night!"

Fear gripped Elijah's heart and he fled into the wilderness. But God took care of him. Queen Jezebel and her soldiers hunted for Elijah but could not find him. The Lord was angry at King Ahab and Queen Jezebel.

The prophet met the king and gave him this message: "The Lord is going to bring great harm to you and sweep you away. You have made Him very angry and have led all of Israel to sin. You and your wife, Queen Jezebel, shall die!"

God's warning came true. King Ahab died in battle against Syria. And after time passed, the Lord told another man, Jehu, "You are to destroy the family of Ahab and avenge the murders of people killed by Jezebel. Dogs shall eat Jezebel at Jezreel, and no one will bury her."

Jehu killed King Jehoram in a field outside the city of Jezreel. Then Jehu rode to the palace. Queen Jezebel painted her eyelids and fixed her hair, then sat at a window to wait for him. When he entered the gate of the palace, Jezebel shouted at him, "How are you today, you murderer!"

Jehu looked up at Jezebel and shouted to the servants who stood on either side of the queen, "Throw her down!"

The men grabbed Jezebel and threw her out of the window. She fell among the horses and was trampled. She died a horrible death in the street.

"This is just what the Lord said would happen," Jehu said.

Jehu killed the remainder of King Ahab and Queen Jezebel's family and their officials and friends. He destroyed the temple of Baal and all of its priests. Nothing was left of the family of the evil King Ahab and Queen Jezebel.

If you want to triumph, listen to God and choose good over evil.

For the wicked shall be destroyed,
but those who trust the Lord
shall be given every blessing.
PSALM 37:9, TLB

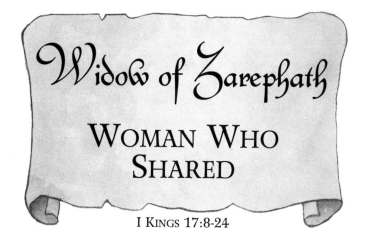

Widow of Zarephath

WOMAN WHO SHARED

I KINGS 17:8-24

ER LEGS AND ARMS TREMBLED with weakness. The poor, starving widow gathered sticks about the yard of her small house. She and her son lived in the city of Zarephath (ZAIR-uh-fath). The widow hardly had strength for her task, but something had urged her to begin preparations for a final meal, for after they ate, there would be no food left for her or her son.

A shadow suddenly fell over her. She turned and saw a stranger—a man almost as worn in appearance as herself. His face, though rugged, seemed trustworthy. He was Hebrew, the widow guessed, perhaps a man of God.

"Might I have a cup of water?" the stranger asked the widow.

Without a word, the widow turned to go fetch water for the man.

"Please bring me a bite of bread too," he called after her.

"I swear by the Lord your God, that I haven't one piece of bread," she replied. "I only have a bit of flour and a little cooking oil. I was gathering sticks to cook the last meal. Then my son and I will die of starvation."

"Make your last meal, but first, make me a small loaf of bread," the stranger told her. "Don't be afraid. The God of Israel promises to give you

111

plenty of flour and oil until He sends rain and the crops grow again."

A surge of hope ran through the widow. Though she was a Gentile, a native of Zidon, and had been raised among worshipers of other gods, she had heard stories of how the mighty God of Israel had rescued and cared for His people, the Israelites. Now it seemed a holy man of God had come to her house. She would not refuse him. She would give him her last bit of food, and by this deed, place her very life under the mercy of God.

The widow mixed the last of the flour with water to make a small loaf of bread. She then baked it using the last of her cooking oil.

"Did you use your last bit of flour and all of your cooking oil?" the man asked her when she brought the loaf to him.

"Yes," the widow replied.

"Go look in your jars again," the man told her.

Hurrying back to the house, the widow was astonished to find the jars she had just emptied filled to their brims with flour and oil!

Crying out in her joy, the widow ran outside to thank the man.

"Don't thank me. I did not do it. The Lord God is the one to thank," he said. "I'm just a prophet of the Lord. My name is Elijah. I am running from Queen Jezebel who wants to kill me because I destroyed the false prophets of Baal. The Lord told me to seek shelter in your house."

"You will always be welcome here, sir," said the widow.

Elijah spent almost three years with the widow and her son. He taught them all about his God. The Lord continued to multiply the flour and the oil. No matter how much they used, there was always plenty left. One day, however, tragedy struck. The widow's son became ill and died.

"O prophet of God!" the widow cried out in her grief. "Have you come here to punish my sins by killing my son?"

"Give him to me," Elijah replied. He carried the boy upstairs to the guest room where he slept and lay him on his bed. "O Lord, why have You taken the son of this good widow who has helped me?" Elijah cried.

He stretched himself over the boy three times and begged the Lord, "O Lord my God, please let him live again!"

The Lord heard Elijah. Suddenly, the little boy stirred with life again. Elijah grabbed him up and rushed down the stairs to the widow.

"Look! He's alive!" he announced to the boy's mother.

"Now I know for sure that you are a prophet," the widow told Elijah happily, "and that everything you have said about the Lord is true!"

When you give your all to God,
He gives even more back to you!

For if you give, you will get!
Your gift will return to you in full
and overflowing measure, pressed down,
shaken together to make room for more,
and running over.
LUKE 6:38A, TLB

Widow and the Pot of Oil
WOMAN WHO PUT FAITH INTO ACTION

II KINGS 4:1-7

ULLING HER SHAWL OVER HER HEAD, the widow ran through the dusty streets to the seminary, a school where young men learned to become teachers of Scripture. The widow's husband had been a student at the seminary and had been taught by Elisha, the prophet. Now the widow was looking desperately for Elisha.

Finding him, she fell at his feet. "Sir, please help me! My husband has died! He owed some money and now the creditor demands that I repay it. If I don't, he will take my two sons as his slaves!"

Elisha helped the widow to her feet. She was trembling with fear.

"Is there anything that you can sell to pay the debt?" asked Elisha.

"No sir, I have nothing of value to sell," the widow shook her head.

"How much food do you have?" Elisha asked.

"Nothing but a jar of olive oil," she replied.

"This is what you should do," Elisha said, a plan from God coming to his mind. "Borrow as many pots and jars from your neighbors as you can. Take your sons into the house and close the door. When you are alone, pour the

olive oil from your jar into the pots and jars you borrowed. The Lord will do a miracle and will multiply your oil so that it will fill every pot!"

The widow stared at him in amazement, then turned and ran home. Calling her sons, she told them to run to the neighbors and borrow as many containers as possible. Then she ran to other neighbors. Before long, she and her sons carried home armfuls of pots, jars, and pans.

As God often prefers to work in quietness and with only one or two of His most humble children, the widow and her sons did not tell anyone what they planned to do.

As their hearts beat with excitement, the widow and her two boys went to the kitchen. Taking up her own small jar of olive oil, the widow silently breathed a prayer and began to pour the oil out into a larger container. She got a funny look on her face and began to laugh as she realized she did not control the flow of oil from the jar. It seemed to flow of its own accord. She could no more stop it than start it flowing.

Her boys gathered around her, and their faces became brighter as they broke into smiles, then into giggles, and then into shouts of joy as the oil kept flowing. Jar after jar and pot after pot was filled and still the oil came! They barely had time to pick up a full pot and replace it with an empty one.

"There are no more pots," the boys finally told their mother.

"Oh!" exclaimed the widow, wondering if the oil would keep flowing anyway and she would have to pour it onto the floor!

The flow of oil immediately stopped, however, and the widow and her two sons happily ran to tell Elisha what had happened.

The prophet beamed with joy when he heard the good news. "God has provided for you," he told them. "You can sell the oil to pay your debt and there will be enough money left over to support all of you for a long time!"

The Lord has an answer for all your problems!

Give your burdens to the Lord.
He will carry them. He will
not permit the godly to slip or fall.
PSALM 55:22, TLB

Shunammite Woman

GRACIOUS GIVER

II KINGS 4:8-37

SITTING IN THE COMFORTABLE living room of her large home in Shunem (SHOO-num), a woman said to her husband, "That man traveling on the road looks weary. He must have traveled some distance. Let's ask him and his servant to dinner."

The woman called to the men and invited them to come inside to eat.

"Thank you," the man said. "I am Elisha and this is my servant, Gehazi. We have traveled from Carmel and are glad to rest for a while."

After they had eaten, Elisha and his servant went on, but after that, whenever they traveled to Shunem, they stopped at the same home to eat.

"I'm sure that Elisha must be a holy prophet," the woman said to her husband. "Let's make a small room for him on the roof. We can put in a bed, table, chair, and an oil lamp and he can rest here whenever he travels by our house."

Elisha was grateful for his resting place in Shunem. One day, while resting in his room, he asked Gehazi, "What could we do for this woman in return for her kindness?"

"She does not have a child," Gehazi answered. "Her husband is much older than she and, most likely, cannot give her children."

Elisha told the woman, "Next year at this time, you shall have a son!"

"O man of God," the woman exclaimed, "do not lie to me!"

But Elisha's words came true. The woman became pregnant and had a baby boy the following year. She and her husband were filled with joy.

One day, however, while playing out in the field, the little boy became sick and died!

"Oh, no!" his mother cried. "Surely, God would not give me this precious child only to have him die so soon. I must go to the prophet Elisha, and ask his help."

She laid her son on Elisha's bed and shut the door. Then, without telling her husband about the boy's death, she saddled a donkey and said to her servant, "We have to go as fast as we can to Mount Carmel. Don't slow down for anything!"

For almost thirty miles, they raced as fast as the donkeys would go. When the woman found Elisha, she fell at his feet in deep anguish. "It was your idea to give me a son! Didn't I say that was impossible, don't lie to me?" she cried out in grief.

The woman did not need to say more. Elisha knew something was wrong with her son.

"Quick! Gehazi, take my staff and hurry to her house. Lay the staff on the child's face," Elisha instructed his servant.

But the woman said to Elisha, "No, I won't go home without you!"

Elisha started home with the woman. Gehazi hurried on ahead and laid Elisha's staff upon the boy, but nothing happened.

When Elisha arrived, he went into the room and shut the door and prayed to the Lord. Then he lay upon the child's body placing his eyes upon the child's eyes, and his hands upon the child's hands. Slowly, the little boy's body began to grow warm! The prophet waited awhile, then stretched over the child again. This time, the boy sneezed seven times and opened his eyes!

Calling the woman into the room, Elisha said, "Here is your son!"

The woman fell down at his feet in thanksgiving. Then, she picked up her little boy and carried him down the stairs.

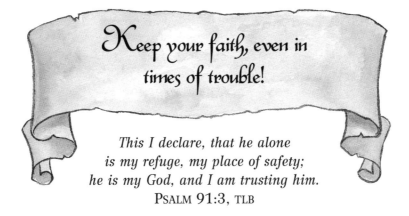

Keep your faith, even in times of trouble!

This I declare, that he alone
is my refuge, my place of safety;
he is my God, and I am trusting him.
PSALM 91:3, TLB

Athaliah
WICKED QUEEN OF JUDAH

II KINGS 11:1;
II CHRONICLES 21:4-6, 18-20; 22:1-10

THE QUEEN OF JUDAH, Athaliah (ath-uh-LIE-uh), looked out as the mourners passed the palace. *How few mourners,* she thought. *Well, we are all better off without him.*

The King of Judah, Jehoram (jih-HOR-um), was dead.

He had been an evil king, murdering his own brothers and worshiping idols. Not many in Jerusalem mourned his death.

His wife, Queen Athaliah, did not mourn for him either. With a cold heart, she had watched him suffer and die. A daughter of the evil King Ahab and wicked Queen Jezebel, Athaliah had grown up surrounded by treachery. She had witnessed the death of her own mother as she was thrown out of a palace window and trampled by horses. Murder and wickedness were commonplace in Athaliah's life. She had been taught only one thing by her infamous royal parents: grab everything you can any way you can get it!

As her son, Ahaziah (ay-huh-ZYE-uh) took the throne of Judah after his father, Athaliah took her place behind the throne and directed her son to walk in the evil ways of her family.

King Ahaziah, however, was killed by Jehu after reigning only one year.

122

This was the man who had also caused the death of Queen Jezebel.

Athaliah was not overly sad about Ahaziah's death. She was more worried about her own place as advisor to the king.

"My son is dead and now one of his sons will want to take over the kingship," she told herself. "My grandsons do not listen to me as did my son, and there are too many of them for me to control. I had better get rid of them quickly before the people try to elect a new king. Then I will rule the kingdom as Queen of Judah!"

Summoning her servants, Athaliah told them to gather all of her grandsons into one room and kill them!

Athaliah grew up in an wicked household and chose to be evil all the days of her life. She never knew the blessing of serving the Lord God of Israel. The evil in her heart caused her to kill even her own grandsons. In the end, she was seized on the palace grounds and put to death.

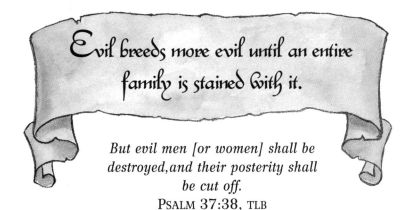

Evil breeds more evil until an entire family is stained with it.

But evil men [or women] shall be destroyed, and their posterity shall be cut off.
PSALM 37:38, TLB

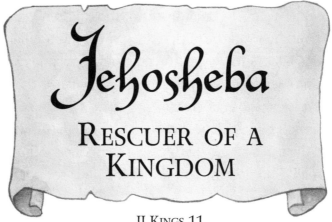

Jehosheba

RESCUER OF A KINGDOM

II KINGS 11

EHOSHEBA (jih-HOSH-uh-buh) AWOKE SUDDENLY, cold terror clutching at her heart. Slipping her robe over her head, she opened the outer door of her sleeping chamber quietly so as not to awaken the other women. She stepped quietly into the hallway that ran from the women's to the children's quarters of the palace. Lights and noises came from the children's rooms. She had an uneasy feeling that something was wrong.

What could be happening to the children at this hour of the night? Jehosheba wondered. She crept down the hallway to get a closer look.

Recently, Jehosheba had married Jehoiada (jih-HOY-uh-duh), the high priest of Judah. Never before had a princess married a high priest and Jehosheba was happy in her marriage. But now, Jehosheba had returned to the palace to stay awhile with her younger sisters, nieces, and nephews. The news of the death of King Ahaziah (Jehosheba's half brother) had thrown the wicked Queen Athaliah into a rampage and everyone was afraid.

"What could she possibly be doing with the children?" Jehosheba asked herself, for she knew this disturbance could only be from Athaliah.

Suddenly, the queen's guard emerged from the children's room, leading two boys by the hand. Jehosheba quickly ducked behind a pillar to avoid being seen. Seconds later, another guard came out, this time carrying a small boy and leading an older one. Puzzled, Jehosheba watched them as they hurried down the corridor and out of sight.

"Those are Ahaziah's sons," Jehosheba said, puzzled. "Now what could the queen want with Ahaziah's sons?" Suddenly, she understood. "Athaliah is going to kill them all! She is going to murder the boys so that no one will take the throne from her!"

Her heart pounding, Jehosheba crept closer to the boys' room and peeked inside. A third guard stood, his back to the door, preventing other boys from escaping.

"O Lord God, what should I do?" Jehosheba prayed frantically. Soon, the guards would return and then they would all be taken and slain! "No, not all," she thought suddenly, a daring plan coming to her mind. She had to move quickly.

Dashing around a corner, Jehosheba silently opened a narrow door used only by the children's servants and nurses. It opened into a small hallway, connected at the rear to the boys' chambers, most likely forgotten by the guards of the queen. Small alcoves or sleeping rooms lay on either side of the hallway, reserved for babies and their nurses. To one of these sleeping rooms Jehosheba hurried, where her nephew, Joash, one-year-old son of King Ahaziah, slept.

Lifting aside the door curtain, Jehosheba slipped into the baby's room, finding his nurse wide awake and frightened. Holding a finger to her lips, Jehosheba picked up the sleeping baby and turned to leave. She motioned for the nurse to follow her.

"Please, Lord, don't let him cry!" Jehosheba prayed. If she were caught by the guards, they would all be killed! Stealthily, creeping back down the hallway and out the little forgotten door, Jehosheba, the baby, and his nurse made their way out of the palace, unseen by any but God.

Running to the temple, Jehosheba hid the baby and his nurse in the temple storeroom. There they lived for six years until finally Queen Athaliah was killed. Joash, at age seven, was set upon the throne.

Joash owed his life and his kingdom to his aunt, Jehosheba. Through her actions, the kingdom of Judah had been redeemed from a wicked ruler.

The actions of just one righteous person can save a kingdom.

So don't be afraid, little flock.
For it gives your Father great
happiness to give you the Kingdom.
LUKE 12:32, TLB

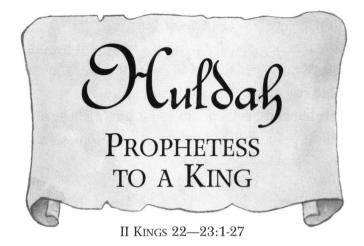

Huldah
PROPHETESS TO A KING

II KINGS 22—23:1-27

ULDAH (HULL-duh) MOVED SLOWLY through the shop turning her head from right to left, overseeing the workers who busily cut, sewed, mended, and altered the many fine garments before them. They took care of the royal wardrobe and Huldah's husband was in charge of the palace tailor shop.

It was an important job, but Huldah was better known for something even more important. She was a prophetess of God. She told God's messages to His people.

This morning, Huldah felt restless. It seemed as if something was about to happen, something important. It wasn't long before she found out what it was. Five tall shadows appeared suddenly in the narrow doorway of the shop, blocking the light.

Looking up, Huldah saw Hilkiah (hil-KEYE-uh), the high priest; Shaphan (SHAY-fun), the king's secretary; Asaiah (ah-SAY-uh), the king's assistant; and two other men.

"We have found a scroll in the temple with God's laws written on it!"

128

Hilkiah, the high priest, told Huldah. "King Josiah (joe-SIGH-uh) read it and became very afraid. The people of Judah have not been following God's laws. The king is afraid that God is very angry with all of us. He commanded us to come to you to find out what the Lord wants us to do."

Huldah looked at the scroll containing God's laws. She knew in her heart that King Josiah was right. The Lord was very angry, for the people of Judah had turned away from Him. Although Josiah was a good king, his father and his grandfather were wicked kings. In fact, Josiah's grandfather, King Manasseh (muh-NASS-uh), had practiced black magic, built heathen shrines and altars, murdered hundreds of innocent people, and had even set up a foreign idol in the Lord's temple! God's commandments had long been forgotten, so that now even the king of God's chosen people had not known His laws nor followed them.

Huldah gravely stared into the eyes of the worried men before her. "Here is a message from the Lord," she said boldly. "Tell the king that I am going to destroy this city and its people just as I stated in the scroll. For the people of Judah have thrown Me aside and have worshiped other gods and have made Me very angry. But because you were sorry and wept before Me, I will listen to your plea. The death of this nation will not occur until after you die."

The men took Huldah's message from the Lord to King Josiah. The king then knew that the scroll was genuine and its words were true. He assembled the people of Judah at the temple and read them the entire scroll filled with God's laws. The people that listened all solemnly promised to obey the Lord and His laws at all times.

The foreign idols, altars, and shrines were destroyed, including the idol that had been placed in the temple. The priests of the Lord returned to Jerusalem and had a Passover celebration so great that people said there had been none like it since the early days of Israel. Never before or after did a king turn so completely to the Lord.

The Lord kept His promise. Even though the kingdom of Judah (and Israel before it) was eventually destroyed, King Josiah and his people, including Huldah the prophetess, enjoyed years of peace and closeness to the Lord. They knew what it meant to walk with Him and to know the fullness of His love and care. Huldah must have felt glad that she had delivered the message that turned the heart of her king, and her nation, back to God.

Be faithful to the Lord even if everyone else falls away.

. . . The Lord will stay with you as long as you stay with him! . . .
II CHRONICLES 15:2, TLB

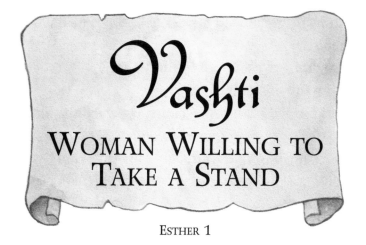

Vashti

WOMAN WILLING TO TAKE A STAND

ESTHER 1

HE PERSIAN KING, Ahasuerus (uh-haz-you-EE-russ), and his officials had been partying for seven days in the royal courtyard of the Shushan Palace. Forever seeking praise of himself, the king basked in the flattery that poured from the lips of his men. There were no women present, except perhaps for the lowly misused concubines of the king.

Now the king's wife, Queen Vashti (VASH-tie), was the most beautiful in the realm. The king, who judged women solely by their outward appearance, decided to show off his beautiful wife to his drunken guests. So he sent his personal aides to bring Queen Vashti to the party.

This is a gross insult to me and to every other woman in the kingdom, the queen thought when she heard the king's order. In that time period, Persian women lived in seclusion and were extremely modest. Such a request of Vashti would be degrading.

"What should I do?" Vashti asked herself. If I refuse the king's order, he may kill me or banish me from the country. However, if I go into the courtyard and allow the drunken men to stare at me and to say nasty things about me, then I would be degraded and humiliated. I have to stand up for what's right and honorable.

Setting her jaw firmly, Vashti looked the king's aides in the eye. "You may tell the king that I refuse his order!"

There was a frightened hush in the courtyard when the aides delivered Vashti's message to the king. No one refused an order of the king!

The king's face turned purple with rage! He turned immediately to his lawyers. "If the queen is allowed to get away with this," they told him, "women everywhere will follow her example. Get rid of her fast!"

The king banished Vashti from his kingdom. He and his lawyers sent a decree throughout the land ordering wives always to obey their husbands.

Vashti held her head high as she left the royal palace. Although the king had won the battle, Vashti had won the war. She had refused to undergo humiliation. She had demonstrated for all to see that self-respect is far more valuable than riches; inner worth far greater than earthly kingships.

Once removed from the sinful palace of the king, perhaps Vashti found true happiness by turning to the one God who treasures the human heart over kingly wealth. He is the one who chooses the weak over the strong. God has promised to put the first last and the last first, and to bring down the ones who raise themselves up at the expense of others. At the end of all things, God's justice will prevail.

Stand firm in what you know is right
and you will never be ashamed.

*Let us turn away from everything
wrong, whether of body or spirit,
and purify ourselves.*
II CORINTHIANS 7:1B, TLB

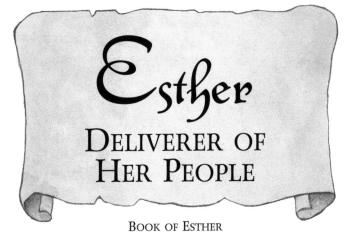

Esther

DELIVERER OF HER PEOPLE

BOOK OF ESTHER

UEEN ESTHER'S HEART beat fast as she made her way down the wide marble hallway of the king's palace. She was afraid. She was going to see the king and she knew that whoever went into the king's inner court without his summons, even the queen herself, was doomed to die unless the king held out his golden scepter.

"No matter the danger, I have to see the king," Esther told her trembling heart. "I have to plead for my people, the Jews. The wicked prime minister, Haman, has ordered that all Jews in the Persian Empire be killed. I must try to stop him. My cousin, Mordecai (MORR-di-keye), has urged me to go before King Ahasuerus to speak for my people. Even if he chooses to kill me, I must go. There is no one else."

Going before the king was not a spur of the moment decision. Esther and her maids had gone without food for three days. They prayed that God would go with Queen Esther and protect her.

This is something I must do, Esther thought. *And if I die, I will have died trying to save my people.*

Gathering all of her courage, Esther left the safety of the hallway and entered the inner court where King Ahasuerus sat upon his royal throne. To her relief, he welcomed her and held out his golden scepter.

"What do you wish, Queen Esther? I will give it to you, even if it is half the kingdom!"

Esther was a wise woman. She did not tell the king what she wanted right away. Instead, she invited the king and Haman, the wicked prime minister, to attend a banquet that she had prepared.

"Now, what is it you wish, my queen?" the king asked Esther after they had finished their meal.

Esther thought for a moment, then decided not to tell the king her wishes. Instead, she invited the king and Haman to another banquet the next day.

That very night King Ahasuerus had trouble sleeping. He decided to read the historical records of his kingdom. In the records, he read how Mordecai, a Jew, had saved the king from an assassination plot.

"I don't think I ever rewarded Mordecai for his action," the king reflected.

In the morning, the king asked Haman, "What should I do to honor a man who truly pleases me?"

The evil prime minister thought the king meant to honor himself, Haman, so he replied eagerly, "Dress the man in your own robes, put him on your own horse, and lead him through the streets of the city, shouting, 'This is the way the king honors those who truly please him!'"

"Let it be done, just as you have said, to Mordecai, the Jew," the king told Haman.

Haman was very angry. He hated Mordecai because Mordecai was a Jew and Mordecai refused to bow down to Haman. He had already built a seventy-five foot gallows on which to hang Mordecai.

That afternoon, King Ahasuerus and Haman attended Queen Esther's second banquet.

"What is your request, Queen Esther?" the king asked her. "Whatever it is,

I will give it to you, even if it is half of my kingdom!"

"Please, Your Majesty, save my life and the lives of my people, for the wicked Haman has plotted against us," Esther told the king.

King Ahasuerus immediately put Haman to death. He was hung on the same gallows he had built to hang Mordecai. Then the king appointed Mordecai as his new prime minister. The plot against the Jews was ended. The king ordered a new decree to be written to protect the Jews and allow them to fight against their enemies.

The Jews were full of joy and gladness. They celebrated with a great time of feasting, and were honored everywhere in Persia.

Every year from that time forward, even to this day, Jewish people celebrate the Feast of Purim. They read the Book of Esther and remember how Esther's courage saved her people from destruction.

Defending the weak is the mark of a true champion.

When God's children are in need, you be the one to help them out.
ROMANS 12:13A, TLB

Gomer

SYMBOL OF UNFAITHFULNESS

HOSEA 1; 3

AN YOU BELIEVE that I am going to marry Hosea, a prophet of God?" Gomer (GO-murr) asked her friends with a laugh. Gomer was a female prostitute, a woman who sleeps with many men. She and her friends laughed at the idea of a prostitute marrying a prophet.

Hosea, however, did not laugh at the idea. God had told him, "Go marry a prostitute because I want to teach your country a lesson. This will be an example of how the people of Israel have been untrue to me. They are like prostitutes when they worship foreign idols."

Hosea married Gomer. She had a son and the Lord said, "Name the child *Jezreel*. I will break the power of Israel in the Valley of Jezreel."

Then Gomer had a daughter. God said, "Name the child *Lo-ruhamah* (low-roo-HAH-muh), meaning 'no more mercy,' for I will have no more mercy on Israel."

After that, Gomer had another son and God said, "Call him *Lo-ammi* (low-AM-eye), meaning 'not my people,' for Israel is not mine and I am not Israel's God."

But Gomer had been unfaithful to Hosea and had run after other men. She had sold her love to them for money, for pretty clothes, and for pleasure. Finally, she became a slave to one of the men.

Then God said, "Because the people of Israel worship idols just like Gomer worships other lovers, I will put an end to Israel's joys and festivals. I will destroy the harvests and the orchards. I will cause a famine and a drought. Just as Gomer chooses to be unfaithful to her husband, so Israel chooses to be unfaithful to God. Just as Gomer believes other men would give her freedom and happiness, so Israel believes other gods will bring freedom and happiness. But that does not prove to be true. As Gomer became a slave, so Israel became a slave to its foreign enemies.

"Go and get your wife again and bring her back to you and love her," God told Hosea. "By this act, I will also show Israel that I will forgive them if they turn their hearts to Me."

With money and grain, Hosea bought back Gomer from the man who had enslaved her. "You must live alone for many days and not go out with other men. I will wait for you to be made pure again," Hosea told Gomer.

Hosea told all these things to the people of Israel, but they did not listen to him. They continued to worship foreign idols and did all kinds of wicked deeds. In God's eyes, Israel was a prostitute just like Gomer.

The story of Gomer was given to us to show that choosing to disobey God and His laws will bring much sadness into our lives. There is no record of what Gomer's feelings were, but the fact that she kept searching for happiness through unfaithfulness would lead us to believe that she was not happy as a wife and mother.

Historical Note

In 722 B.C., the northern kingdom of Israel was defeated by Assyria and the people put into slavery. The southern kingdom of Judah remained free for a while, but then, in 586 B.C., it was overcome by the Babylonians and its people enslaved. God's warning had come true! Israel did become a slave.

Fifty years later, however, God caused the Persian king, Cyrus, to allow the people of Judah to return to Jerusalem to rebuild the temple and the city. This fulfilled God's promise to Hosea that He would continue to love His people even though they had been unfaithful to Him.

Remaining true to God brings His protection in your life.

Oh, love the Lord, all of you who are his people; for the Lord protects those who are loyal to him, but harshly punishes all who haughtily reject him.
PSALM 31:23, TLB

All scholars do not agree on the details of the story of Hosea and Gomer. We have, to the best of our ability, presented the story as we interpret it in God's Word, the Bible.

Women of the New Testament

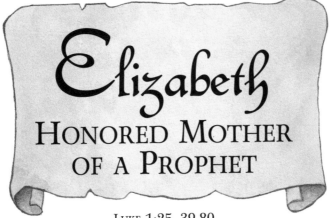

Elizabeth
HONORED MOTHER OF A PROPHET

LUKE 1:25, 39-80

ACHARIAS'S (zack-uh-REYE-us-es) FINGERS TREMBLED as he lit the incense on the altar in the temple. Outside, the crowd of worshipers prayed. Suddenly, before Zacharias's eyes, an angel appeared!

"Don't be afraid," the angel said, "for I am here to tell you that your wife, Elizabeth (ee-LIZ-uh-beth), will have a son. His name shall be John. He will be a great prophet of the Lord and will prepare the people for the coming of the Messiah!"

"But that's impossible!" Zacharias exclaimed. "My wife and I are too old to have a baby."

"I am Gabriel and God Himself sent me to you with this message," the angel replied. "Because you did not believe me, you are to be stricken silent and unable to speak until the child is born!"

Not long afterwards, Elizabeth became pregnant. "How wonderful!" Elizabeth exclaimed. "The Lord is so kind to give us a child."

Elizabeth was so excited at the thought of having a baby for her very own. She was not as young as the other mothers, and she may have worried that

she might not have the strength to take care of a toddler. But God had proclaimed the baby's birth, and so she put her trust in Him that everything would work out all right.

One day, when Elizabeth was six months pregnant, a special visitor knocked on her door.

"Greetings, Elizabeth!" the visitor announced, rushing into her arms. It was Mary, Elizabeth's relative from Nazareth. At the sound of Mary's greeting, Elizabeth's child leaped inside of her.

"Oh, Mary!" Elizabeth exclaimed. "You are favored by God. I am honored that the mother of my Lord should visit me! Because you believed that God would do what He said, He has given you this wonderful blessing!"

Mary stayed with Elizabeth about three months. By that time, Elizabeth's baby boy was born, just as the angel had said. Many relatives and friends came to see the baby and rejoice over the miracle God had given to Elizabeth and Zacharias.

"Surely, you will name the baby Zacharias after his father," the visitors said to Elizabeth.

"No, he shall be named John," Elizabeth answered.

"What?" they all exclaimed. "There is no one in your family named John. Let's ask the father what he thinks."

The people asked Zacharias what he wanted to name the baby. Zacharias wrote on a tablet, "His name is John." Instantly, Zacharias could speak again.

"Praise God! He is sending us a mighty Savior from the line of David, as He promised long ago. You, my little son, shall be a prophet of God and shall prepare the way for the Messiah. You will tell people how to find salvation through the forgiveness of their sins."

Elizabeth loved and cherished her son, never forgetting the miracle of his birth. She taught him all she knew of the Lord. The little boy grew to greatly love God.

When John grew up, he went out to the wilderness to live and begin his public ministry. The Bible says that he ate locusts and wild honey, and that he preached, "Repent, for the kingdom of God is at hand." He proclaimed the coming of the Messiah, leading the people to repent of their sins and baptizing them in the Jordan River. In this way, he became known as John the Baptist.

It must have been an awesome feeling for Elizabeth to know that her son would prepare the hearts of people to receive the Good News of salvation.

Even the greatest of men begin with the nurture and care of a mother.

. . . Anything is possible if you have faith.
MARK 9:23, TLB

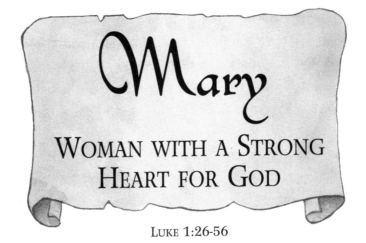

Mary

WOMAN WITH A STRONG HEART FOR GOD

LUKE 1:26-56

EARFULLY, Mary stared at the stranger who had suddenly appeared before her. He was no ordinary person. His body was outlined in a glow of light that shimmered whenever he moved. Instantly, Mary knew that he was an angel.

"Hello, Mary," the angel said. "You have pleased God! He is with you always."

Mary's mouth opened in surprise. Had the angel really spoken to her? What did he mean? Confused and frightened, Mary took a step backward.

"Do not be afraid, Mary," the angel said kindly. "God wants to give you a great blessing. Soon, you will become pregnant and have a baby boy. You should name Him Jesus. He will be great and will be called the Son of God."

"But how can I become pregnant?" Mary gasped. "I have never been married and I have never slept with a man."

"You will become pregnant through God and His Holy Spirit," the angel answered. "That way, the baby Jesus will be holy."

Wow! I am to be the mother of God's own Son, the Messiah, Mary thought, *but what if other people don't understand? My own family might get angry at*

me for becoming pregnant before I am actually married. Joseph, the man I am to marry, might think I am a bad person and never want to see me again.

Mary frowned at her troubled thoughts. No, she told herself firmly. I will not worry. Surely, the Lord will take care of everything. I will trust in Him.

"I am the Lord's servant," Mary said. "May it all come true as you have said."

Soon afterwards, Mary visited her relative, Elizabeth. The angel had told Mary that Elizabeth was going to have a baby, even though she was too old and had never had a baby before!

"Oh, Mary!" Elizabeth exclaimed, "as soon as I heard your voice, the baby inside of me leaped for joy! You are receiving God's favor. You have always believed in His promises. That is why He has graciously chosen you to be the mother of His Son."

"I am amazed that God picked me for this honor," Mary told Elizabeth. "I am just a girl. I am not rich. I am not important. Yet God chose me. Now people for generations to come will know my name and call me blessed."

Mary danced happily around the room. "Elizabeth, isn't it neat that God works His miracles through unimportant people like me? He doesn't choose people who think they are more important than others. God chooses the smaller, weaker people—ones who have true love in their hearts. My heart is strong for the Lord and that is more important than bodily strength.

"Yes, I believe in God's promises. Today, He has kept His biggest promise to Israel—sending Jesus, the Messiah. I am going to be part of that promise. Oh, I can't wait to see what God is going to do next in my life!"

Believing in God's promises builds strong faith and a strong heart.

For the Lord is faithful to his promises.
ISAIAH 30:18B, TLB

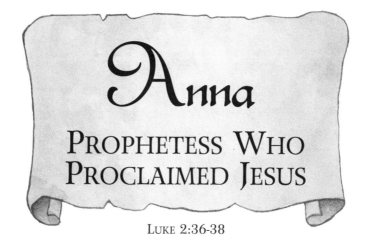

Anna

PROPHETESS WHO PROCLAIMED JESUS

LUKE 2:36-38

EAR LORD, send your Messiah soon!" Anna prayed. She had prayed the same prayer over and over for so many years. Anna was now an old woman! She was eighty-four years old. Her husband had died years ago, and Anna had placed herself in the service of the Lord. She went to the temple every day to worship God by praying and often fasting. Anna was a prophetess, one through whom God proclaims His messages to others.

Rising up slowly from her aged knees, Anna grasped a pillar for support. Pausing to catch her breath, she wondered at the rapid beating of her heart and the fluttery feeling in her stomach. It was not old age that made her feel that way, but rather an excitement that had been growing upon her all week. Something important was about to happen!

As a prophetess of God, Anna had often delivered messages from God to His people. Then she would feel the excitement of being chosen by God, of being touched by God, and of hearing His very words deep within her mind. But this time it was different. The excitement was even more profound.

Shaking her head, Anna walked toward the inner court of the temple

where she recognized the familiar figure of Simeon, a man, who like herself, spent much time at the temple in prayer. Simeon now stood before a young husband and wife. In Simeon's arms was a baby.

A sudden flash of insight struck Anna as she gazed at the young couple and the baby in Simeon's arms. Moving closer, she heard Simeon say, "Now Lord, I can die content for I have seen the Savior You have given to the world!"

As if spellbound, Anna moved to Simeon's side and looked at the young couple named Mary and Joseph. Then she gazed at the infant, Jesus. Instantly, a look of wondrous joy spread across her face!

"It is He! It is the Messiah!" she cried out loud, tears flowing down her cheeks. "Oh, thank You, Lord, for showing me Your Son!"

Now she understood the excitement that had been building inside of her. This was the best day of her life! Despite her age, Anna ran to tell everyone in Jerusalem that the Messiah had finally arrived!

Don't give up! At the right time, God will answer your prayers!

I waited patiently for God to help me; then he listened and heard my cry.
PSALM 40:1, TLB

Woman of Samaria
ONE WHO BROUGHT HER PEOPLE TO CHRIST

JOHN 4:4-42; ACTS 8:5-8

HE SAMARITAN WOMAN wearily set her water pot down beside the well. It was a hot day and she had walked far. A stranger sat beside the well. By His dress, the woman could tell He was a Jew. Jews never spoke to Samaritans. They believed Samaritans were unclean and inferior to the Jews. So she was surprised when the stranger asked her for a drink. Even though they were considered enemies, the woman drew water for Him. She didn't realize she was talking to Jesus.

"Why do You, a Jew, ask me, a Samaritan woman, for a drink?" she asked.

"If only you knew what a wonderful gift God has for you and who I am, you would ask Me for some living water!" the man replied.

"But you don't have a rope or a water pot and this is a very deep well," the woman said. "How would you get any living water? Besides, this is Jacob's well. How can you find water better than this?"

"Anyone who drinks the water from this well will soon become thirsty," He said, "but whoever drinks My water, will never thirst again. The water I give is like a constant spring that waters people forever with eternal life."

"Please sir," the woman said eagerly, "give me Your water so that I'll never be thirsty again and won't have to walk to the well every day!"

"First, go and get your husband," the man told her.

"But I am not married," the woman answered.

"You have spoken the truth," the man nodded, "for you have had five husbands and you are now living with a man who is not your husband!"

The woman gasped. "You must be a prophet! Tell me, why do Jews say that Jerusalem is the only place to worship, while Samaritans believe we should worship at Mount Gerazim where our fathers worshiped?"

"It does not really matter where we worship, but it's how we worship that counts," the man replied. "God looks for people who worship Him in truth. But the Jews have been shown more about God than the Samaritans, for it is through the Jews that salvation will come."

"Well, at least I know that the Messiah will come someday," the woman said, "and when He does, He will explain everything to us!"

"I am the Messiah!" the man told her.

Just then, the disciples of Jesus arrived at the well. They were surprised to see their Master talking to a woman, let alone a Samaritan woman.

The woman herself was so surprised at Jesus' words that she ran to her village, leaving behind her water pot!

"Come and meet a man who was able to tell me all about my life!" the woman told everyone in the village. "Could this be the Messiah?"

After hearing the woman's report, many of the people of the village believed that Jesus was the Messiah. They hurried to the well to see Him. They begged Him to stay at their village and He stayed there for two days, long enough for many more to hear Him and believe in Him.

Jesus chose the woman as the first Samaritan to announce the coming of the Messiah to her people. Because of her witness, others came to know Jesus, and some years later, when Philip the Evangelist came to preach to the Samaritans, their hearts were ready to hear of the resurrection of Jesus. This news brought great joy to Samaria.

God chooses the lowly and through them does His greatest tasks.

He gives power to the tired and worn out, and strength to the weak.
ISAIAH 40:29, TLB

DOORS OPENED AND CLOSED and voices echoed through the house as family and friends returned home from the synagogue. The old woman stirred in her bed, awakened out of a fitful sleep. Slowly, she raised her hand to her forehead. It was hot and clammy while every other part of her body was chilled.

"If I am to die, please take me in a hurry so that no one has to care for me," the woman prayed. Because her husband had died several years ago, she lived with her married daughter and her son-in-law, Peter, the fisherman. Peter's brother, Andrew, also lived with them. The house was lively and always full of children, nieces, nephews, aunts, and uncles. The old woman cared for all of them and they loved her dearly.

Suddenly, outside her bedroom, footsteps sounded.

"Oh dear," the woman sighed. She felt too sick to talk to anyone.

A soft knock and the door opened slowly. The woman was relieved to see only the head of her daughter peek into the room. But then, to her deep

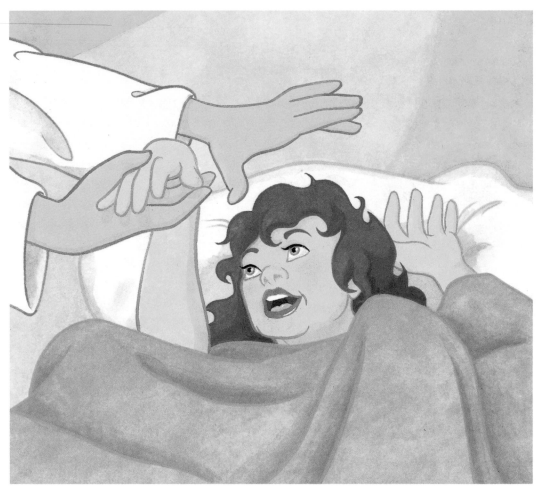

distress, the door opened to admit Peter and another man into the room!

The woman's eyes widened as she stared at the man who stood at the foot of her bed. It was Jesus, the Teacher from Galilee! As she stared at the warm understanding in Jesus' face, the woman's embarrassment swiftly melted away. She did not even notice that a crowd had gathered in the doorway. She had eyes only for Jesus.

Jesus moved to the side of her bed. Speaking soft words of comfort meant only for her ears, He leaned over her and gently grasped her hand.

Immediately, a new strength flowed into her.

As Jesus helped her to sit up, her fever left completely. Sickness and weariness left her body. Indeed, renewed vitality flowed through her limbs. She felt as if she could jump and shout for joy!

"Oh thank You, Master," she said and then found to her wonder that tears flowed freely down her face.

He smiled and patted her hand, and then He and the others were gone from the room. Only her daughter remained.

"Where are my clothes?" the woman asked, throwing off the bed covers.

"Oh Mother! You should rest some more. You are getting up too quickly!" her daughter replied.

"Nonsense! I've never felt better in my life!" the older woman beamed. "Peter and Andrew are right to follow after Jesus. Look how He has healed me! He must be a special prophet of God!"

"I think He might be even more special than that," her daughter answered with a smile.

"I think so, too." Her mother squeezed her arm. Then she got dressed and hurried downstairs to prepare a special dinner for Jesus, the man who had healed her.

When you are down, Jesus will give you new strength to rise again.

. . . I am your God. I will strengthen you; I will help you; I will uphold you with my victorious right hand.
ISAIAH 41:10, TLB

Widow of Nain
A GRATEFUL MOTHER

LUKE 7:11-17

THE ROAD leading to the city of Nain was steep and rocky. On each side of the road stood burial caves where the citizens of Nain brought their dead wrapped in linen sheets to be buried.

Jesus and His followers climbed the steep road, passed the burial caves, and had nearly reached the city gates when a funeral procession emerged. A young man had died, the only child of a widow.

The widow stumbled along after the men who carried her son's body which was placed on a flat stretcher.

"Oh, my son," she sobbed. "My only son. What will I do without him?" The widow wept bitterly. Not only had her son's life been dear to her, but also he had been the only one to support her. She now faced starvation without his loving provision.

Jesus gazed at the widow and His heart was filled with compassion.

"Don't cry," He told her in a strong but gentle voice. Then He stepped towards the body.

The procession stopped as everyone watched in amazement to see Jesus

158

reach out His hand and touch the cold, lifeless body of the young man. The people of Israel believed that a rabbi would be contaminated if he touched a dead body, and Jesus was known as a rabbi.

But then, Jesus did an even more amazing thing. He spoke to the young man. "Arise!" Jesus commanded.

Immediately, the young man sat up. He tore off the covering placed about his mouth and began to talk to the people that stood around him!

"Ohhhhh!" the widow cried out and now she wept tears of joy.

Jesus lifted the young man off the funeral stretcher and gave him into his mother's arms. This was the first time that Jesus had raised a person from the dead and He had done so to heal a mother's grief-stricken heart!

"Oh, thank You!" the widow choked through her tears. Her face shone with wonder. She had never met Jesus before; yet He loved her enough to give back her son from the dead!

"We have seen a miracle from God today!" the crowd exclaimed. Reports of what Jesus had done spread throughout Judea and even across its borders.

God's love for you is beyond measure.

Long ago, even before
he made the world,
God chose us to be his very own. . . .
EPHESIANS 1:4, TLB

160

Sinful Woman in the House of Simon
WOMAN SET FREE!

LUKE 7:36-50

A S SOON AS THE WOMAN ENTERED Simon's house, all eyes looked at her with hatred. They looked down on her because she had made some bad choices and lived a sinful life. Men often visited her at night, bringing her costly presents if she would sleep with them. The guests in Simon's house were all religious men—Pharisees—eager to point out other people's sins, but never admitting to their own.

Clutched in the woman's hand was one such costly gift, a beautiful bottle filled with expensive perfume.

Looking about, her eyes found the one for whom she was searching— Jesus! His eyes met hers and her heart melted in the warmth and tenderness of His gaze. Though many men had told her they loved her, it was only her body they had loved. But Jesus was different. Here was a man who had never touched her, yet loved her completely. His were the only eyes in the room that did not condemn her.

Going to Jesus, she knelt at His feet and began to cry. Her tears would not stop. She washed His feet with her tears and dried them with her hair.

She kissed His feet and poured the perfume upon them.

Simon, a self-righteous Pharisee, watched the woman with disgust. He wondered how she had entered his house and how he was going to get her out without making a scene in front of his guests.

This proves that Jesus is not a prophet, Simon said to himself. *If God had really sent Him, Jesus would know she was a bad woman!*

Jesus suddenly turned to Simon and said, "There once was a man who loaned money to two people—$5,000 to one and $500 to the other. Neither person could pay him back so he kindly forgave both of them, letting them keep the money! Which person do you think loved him the most?"

"I suppose the one who owed him the most," Simon answered.

"Correct," Jesus agreed. "When I entered your home, you didn't give Me water to wash the dust from My feet, but this woman here has washed them with her tears and dried them with her hair. You did not give Me the customary kiss of greeting, but this woman has kissed My feet many times. You did not give Me olive oil to cool and cleanse My head, but she has covered My feet with rare perfume! This woman has many sins, but they are all forgiven because she has loved Me very much; but someone who is forgiven little shows little love."

The woman stared at Jesus. Had she heard Him correctly?

"Your sins are forgiven," Jesus said to her.

Immediately, the men around him began to grumble. "Who does Jesus think He is, going around forgiving sins?"

The woman ignored the men. Staring into the Savior's eyes, she knew the truth about Him.

Jesus smiled at her. "Your faith has saved you. Go in peace!"

The woman jumped to her feet. She was free! Her sins were forgiven! Walking happily out of the door, the woman was the only one set free that day in the house of Simon.

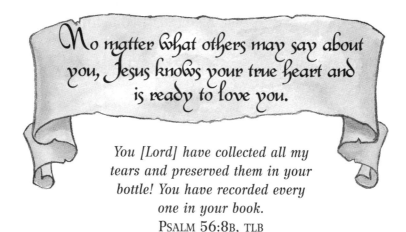

No matter what others may say about you, Jesus knows your true heart and is ready to love you.

You [Lord] have collected all my tears and preserved them in your bottle! You have recorded every one in your book.
PSALM 56:8B, TLB

Woman with an Issue of Blood
DAUGHTER OF FAITH

MARK 5:22-34; LUKE 8:43-48

"PLEASE, MASTER, come home with me! My little girl is dying! Come and place Your hands on her and make her well," cried a man who had fallen at Jesus' feet. It was Jairus, the rabbi of a local synagogue.

Jesus agreed to go with Jairus and began to make His way through the crowds. It seemed that everyone in Judea had come to see Jesus. The people pressed in on Him closely.

Suddenly, Jesus halted. "Who touched Me?" He asked loudly.

"Master, everyone is crowding up against You," said Peter, one of Jesus' disciples. "Many are touching You. . . ."

"No, someone deliberately touched Me," Jesus answered. "I felt healing power go out from Me."

Turning, His eyes searched the crowd and fell upon a certain woman. Trembling, she fell to her knees. "I am the one who touched You," she told Him. "I have been bleeding inside for twelve years and have spent all my money on doctors, but still have not been cured. I have heard about You and the wonderful miracles You perform. I

thought that if I could just touch Your clothing, I would be healed."

Jesus looked down upon her with love in His eyes. He knew that this woman had suffered physically for many years. He also knew that because of her bleeding, she had been pronounced "unclean" by the religious leaders, and prevented from normal contact with others and even from worship in the synagogue.

"Daughter," Jesus addressed her in an endearing manner, "your faith has made you well. Go in peace and be healed of your disease!"

The woman jumped up with a strength she had not known for twelve years. Her face shone and her whole body radiated a healthy happiness. Not only was she healed, but she had looked upon the Messiah, Jesus!

Put your faith in God and He will come through for you.

What is faith? It is the confident assurance that something we want is going to happen.
HEBREWS 11:1A, TLB

Jairus's Daughter

CHILD WHO REJOICED

MARK 5:22-24, 38-42;
LUKE 8:41, 42, 49-56

"T HERE IS NO USE troubling the Teacher now," the messenger told Jairus, "your little girl is dead!"

Jairus cried out in anguish. He had found Jesus in a crowd of people and had asked Him to come heal his twelve-year-old daughter. But before they could reach the house, his little girl had died!

"Don't be afraid," Jesus said. "Trust Me and she will be all right."

Hurrying to the house, they found it full of people weeping loudly. "Stop crying!" Jesus told them. "The girl is not dead. She is only asleep!"

The people laughed at Him. They all knew she was dead.

Going into the girl's bedroom, Jesus took only the girls' parents and His disciples—Peter, James, and John—with Him. Taking hold of the girl's hand, Jesus called to her, "Get up, little girl!"

To everyone's amazement, life returned immediately to her body and the girl jumped up out of bed.

Crying and laughing with joy, her parents hugged her and held her

tight. "Thank You!" they said through their tears to Jesus.

Jesus smiled. "Give your daughter something to eat right away," He advised them. "Please don't tell anyone how I raised her from the dead."

Jesus was afraid that if news of His miracles spread too fast, the religious leaders—the Pharisees and the Sadducees—would try to kill Him before He had a chance to do everything God wanted Him to do on earth. These men hated Jesus because He pointed out their falseness to the people. They refused to believe He was the Messiah.

But at least one religious leader believed in Jesus, and that was Jairus, the rabbi of a local synagogue. Jesus had just raised his daughter from the dead. Jairus and his family would always remember the special blessing they had received from the hands of the Messiah!

Though others may speak against Him, believing in Jesus is the only way to heaven!

Then he asked them,
"Who do you think I am?"
Simon Peter answered,
"The Christ, the Messiah, the
Son of the living God."
MATTHEW 16:15, 16, TLB

Salome

DANCER WHO BROUGHT DEATH

MARK 6:17-28

ITHOUT WAITING FOR HER MAID, Salome (suh-LOW-me) pulled her new outfit over her head and looked at herself in the mirror. The change was startling. No longer did she look like a young girl, barely out of childhood and into her teens. In this outfit, she looked at least sixteen years old!

"Oh, Mother, it's beautiful!" Salome cried happily as her mother, Queen Herodias (heh-ROH-dee-us), entered Salome's dressing chamber.

Herodias smiled at Salome's lovely reflection in the mirror, and Salome was glad to see her mother smile again. Lately, the queen had been angry against a prophet called John the Baptist. It seemed that John had criticized King Herod for marrying Herodias. Herod had stolen Herodias away from her first husband, Philip, who was actually Herod's own brother! Herod had then divorced his first wife to marry Herodias.

John the Baptist said it was a sin for Herod to marry Herodias. King Herod had imprisoned John for speaking against the king and queen; but to the queen's frustration, the king refused to execute the prophet. For some reason, Herod seemed to like John the Baptist and had even begun to listen to

him. Herodias was afraid John might convince King Herod to abandon her. Then she and Salome would be put out of the palace with no where to go and no place to live.

Why doesn't old John the Baptist mind his own business? Salome thought to herself. *Who cares what a dirty man who lives in caves and eats locusts thinks anyway!*

"Be sure to be ready on time tonight," the queen broke in on Salome's thoughts. "You must not keep the king waiting."

Nervous excitement flowed through Salome. It was King Herod's birthday and tonight she was to dance at his birthday feast!

That evening, Salome waited behind a screen in the banquet hall until the palace musicians began to play their instruments. Swallowing her nervousness, she began to dance in slow, steadied movements working into sways and swirls, the pace constantly rising and falling in intricate movements. At the end, the male guests (for only men had been invited to the party) loudly expressed their approval. Salome, her face flushed, bowed low before her stepfather, King Herod.

"Ask me for anything you desire," the king vowed to Salome in front of his guests, "and I will give it to you, even if it is half of my kingdom!"

Surprised and flattered, Salome rushed out of the room to consult her mother. "What should I ask for?" she asked Queen Herodias.

Without hesitation, Herodias replied, "Ask for the head of John the Baptist to be brought to you immediately on a platter!"

Startled, Salome stepped backward, away from her mother. It seemed such a dreadful thing to do at a banquet. Inwardly, she felt afraid, but she knew better than to argue with the queen.

Returning to Herod, Salome made her request and watched the king's face recoil at her words. She knew he regretted his offer, but he could not break his oath in front of his guests.

Salome waited nervously as the king ordered his servants to perform the grisly deed. They soon returned bearing a platter. Salome turned pale and turned her head as she took the platter from a servant and carried it out of the banquet room to her waiting mother. For Salome, the happy night had turned to tragedy. Little had she known that her birthday dance would become a dance of death for the prophet, John the Baptist.

An evil act never solves anything, but only makes things worse.

Don't let evil get the upper hand but conquer evil by doing good.
ROMANS 12:21, TLB

Syro-Phoenician Woman
DETERMINED SEEKER OF HELP

MATTHEW 15:21-28; MARK 7:24-30

THE WOMAN STRODE from her house up the dusty road toward a group of Jewish travelers. For a brief moment, the woman's courage failed. Some of the Jews hated her people, residents of the coastal cities of Tyre and Sidon. They called them heathen Gentiles and idol worshipers. Yet the woman had no choice. She had to approach these Jews and fall at the feet of the one they called Jesus to plead for the healing of her young daughter. Yes, even in her country, people had heard of the miracles of Jesus.

As soon as she came near to Jesus, she knew that the stories about Him were true. He looked at her with recognition in His eyes as if He already knew her and all about her request.

"Lord, have mercy on me," the woman pleaded, falling at Jesus' feet. "My daughter has a demon within her and it torments her constantly."

The woman waited for Jesus to speak but He did not say a word. He did not refuse her request or walk away from her.

"Tell this woman to leave," the male disciples said harshly. "She is bothering us with her begging."

"I was sent to help the lost sheep of Israel, not to help the Gentiles," Jesus said to the woman.

"Please sir, help me!" she cried. She had no intentions of giving up, since the well-being of her daughter was at stake!

"First, I should help the Jews," Jesus replied. "It doesn't seem right to take bread from the children and throw it to the dogs."

"Oh yes it is," the woman quickly replied, "for even the puppies beneath the table are given scraps from the children's plates!"

"Good! You have answered well!" Jesus told the woman with a smile. "Your faith is large and your request is granted. Go on home. Your little girl is healed."

Hurrying home, the woman found her daughter lying quietly in bed, completely healed. Smiling, the woman thought back to her words with Jesus. He had seemed pleased with her determination and her answers. Had He been testing her, or had there been another reason? Perhaps Jesus had wanted His disciples to see that He had come for everyone, not just the people of Israel.

The woman shrugged her shoulders. Whatever the reason, her little girl had been healed. She now knew that the claims about Jesus were true and she would believe in Him all of her life!

Determined people please God!

Ask, and you will be given what you ask for. Seek, and you will find. Knock, and the door will be opened.
MATTHEW 7:7, TLB

Woman Accused of Adultery
ACCUSED, BUT NO LONGER GUILTY!

JOHN 8:1-11

T HE MEN DRAGGED her through the streets of Jerusalem, twisting her arms and bruising her feet and ankles. Her hair flew about wildly. Her clothing tore. She became smudged and dirty with the dust of the street.

What were they doing? Where were they taking her? The woman glanced swiftly at her tormentors. They were all rabbis and Pharisees, men who thought that they were keepers of the law, and quickly pounced on any lesser person who did not follow it to the letter.

Forcing her to climb a column of steps, the angry men brought her to the temple and threw her down in front of a crowd of people who had come to listen to Jesus.

"Teacher," one of the angry men addressed Jesus loudly, "this woman was caught in the act of adultery. Moses' law says to stone her! What do You say?"

The leaders were trying to trap Jesus. If He told them to go ahead and stone the woman, He would be looked upon as cruel and His reputation as tender and forgiving to sinners would be spoiled. But if He told them to let her go, Jesus would anger many people who claimed to be defenders of the law.

A great silence fell. The woman cringed, feeling the condemning eyes of the crowd upon her. She waited for Jesus' answer, certain that He, too, would stare at her with hate-filled eyes and sentence her to death by stoning. After all, these religious people were hypocrites and frauds. They cited the law and yet did not follow it entirely themselves.

The law of Moses decreed that the woman's partner in adultery—the man—be tried and also put to death with the woman. But, where was the man? The leaders had not bothered to accuse him. Instead, they had singled her out, and she was unable to fight back. They had damaged her reputation by accusing her in front of a crowd of people, and now were eager to stone her to death.

The woman waited, the Pharisees waited, and the crowd waited; still Jesus did not answer. In fact, He did not even look at them, but stooped down and wrote in the dust with His finger.

"Speak up! What do You say to our question?" the leaders asked Him, angry at the way Jesus ignored them.

Finally, Jesus stood up and looked at them. "All right, hurl the stones at her until she dies, but only he who has never sinned may throw the first stone!"

The woman looked up in surprise. What did Jesus say? She looked at the faces of the leaders. Guilt was written all over them. They knew that they had committed many kinds of sins.

One by one, beginning with the oldest and highest in office, the leaders backed off and sneaked away. At last, only the woman remained to stand before Jesus. She did not run or try to hide from Him. He had defended her against her accusers with great wisdom and compassion. She had never known such respect as the Teacher of Galilee showed to her that day.

After all the religious leaders had left, Jesus again stood up and said to the woman, "Where are your accusers? Didn't even one of them stay to condemn you?"

"No sir," she answered.

"Neither do I condemn you," Jesus told her. "Go and sin no more."

Remembering our own shortcomings helps us to forgive others.

And why worry about a speck in the eye of a brother when you have a board in your own?
MATTHEW 7:3, TLB

Mary of Bethany
WOMAN WHO RECOGNIZED QUALITY

MARK 14:3-9; LUKE 10:38-42;
JOHN 12:1-8

EXCITEDLY, Mary listened to the man called Jesus who had come to stay at her house. He and His disciples were traveling through Bethany on their way to Jerusalem. Ever since her older sister, Martha, had brought them home, Mary had been unable to contain her joy. Now the house was full of strangers, disciples of Jesus.

Holding onto every word He spoke, Mary wondered if this could indeed be the Messiah of Israel as some had whispered. Jesus certainly seemed extraordinary, different than any other man Mary had ever known, including her brother, Lazarus. And He told the most marvelous stories!

Suddenly, the grating voice of her sister, Martha, dashed Mary's happiness. "Sir, doesn't it seem unfair to you that my sister, Mary, just sits here while I do all the work?" Martha complained to Jesus. "Tell her to come and help me!"

Her face flushed, Mary stared at the floor guiltily. Perhaps she should have been helping her sister with the big dinner she was preparing for the guests. But she just couldn't tear herself away from Jesus. Now, she was going to get in trouble in front of everybody! Of course, Jesus would agree with Martha. Everybody agreed with Martha!

"Martha, dear friend," Jesus replied gently, "you are so upset over all the little things. There is really only one thing to be concerned about here and Mary has discovered it. I won't take it away from her!"

Surprised, Mary looked up and found Jesus smiling down at her, filling her heart with sunshine. She was not to be banished to the kitchen. Jesus wanted her to stay and listen to Him. Yes, she had discovered the one thing to be concerned about—Jesus! But she had also discovered something else: she was important to Him!

Mary saw quite a bit of Jesus. He and His followers oftentimes stayed at her house and they became good friends. Then, one day, shortly before Jesus' death, when Jesus was eating dinner at the home of Simon the leper, Mary broke a bottle of perfume and poured it on Jesus' head.

People around them became upset. "What a waste!" they cried. "She could have sold that perfume for much money and given it to the poor!"

But Jesus said, "Leave her alone! Don't get after her for doing something good. You will always have the poor among you and they will need your help, but I won't be here much longer! She has done the best she could and has anointed My body ahead of time for burial. Truly, whenever the Gospel is preached throughout the world, people will remember what Mary has done here tonight and will praise her for it!"

Discover what's truly important
and then go for it!

But seek first His kingdom and
His righteousness; and all these things
shall be added to you.
MATTHEW 6:33, NASB

Martha
WOMAN WHO CHANCED TO BELIEVE

JOHN 11:1-45

ARTHA SLIPPED away from the friends who crowded into her living room. They gathered around Mary, her sister, who had cried without ceasing since their brother, Lazarus, had died four days ago.

Hurrying out the door, Martha ran to the main road. She spotted a small group of travelers and quickly ran to them.

"Master!" she cried, reaching Jesus. "If You had only been here, my brother would not have died. Yet, even now, I know that God would do whatever You ask Him to!"

"I am the one who raises the dead and gives them life again," Jesus said. "Whoever believes in Me, even if that one should die, shall live again. People are given eternal life for believing in Me. Do you believe this, Martha?"

"Yes, Master," Martha replied, "I believe You are the Messiah, the Son of God, the one for whom we have waited."

Jesus looked long into Martha's eyes. He seemed pleased with her reply. Martha was comforted to have such a friend.

Martha hurried back to the house and called Mary.

But when their friends saw the sisters leave the house, they thought they were going to Lazarus's tomb to weep and decided to follow them.

When Mary reached Jesus, she fell down at His feet and cried, "Master, if You had been here, my brother would still be alive!"

"Where is he buried?" Jesus asked.

"Come and see," the sisters answered.

Tears came to Jesus' eyes as He walked with the sisters.

"See how much Jesus loved Lazarus," some of the people said. But others said, "If He could heal a blind man, why couldn't He have kept Lazarus from dying?"

Soon they reached Lazarus' tomb. It was a cave with a heavy stone rolled across the opening.

"Roll the stone aside," Jesus said.

"He has been dead four days!" Martha exclaimed. "By now, the smell will be terrible!"

Jesus looked at Martha tenderly. "But didn't I tell you that you will see something wonderful from God if you believe?"

Martha looked deep into the eyes of her Savior. She saw love and sympathy, but she also saw something more. In the eyes of Jesus was a challenge. Would Martha take a chance, in front of all these people, and believe that Jesus, the Messiah, could perform a miracle beyond all miracles, one for which Martha hardly dared to hope?

"Yes!" she nodded, and the men pushed away the heavy stone.

Looking up to heaven, Jesus prayed out loud. "Father, thank You for hearing Me. I know You always hear Me, but I say this so these people will believe You sent Me." Then Jesus shouted, "LAZARUS! COME OUT!"

Clutching Mary's hand tightly, Martha watched a figure emerge from the tomb. It was Lazarus, wrapped from head to toe in grave clothes!

"Unwrap him and let him go!" ordered Jesus.

Martha laughed in delight as she looked upon her brother standing before her whole, healthy, and blinking in the bright sunlight. Jesus had done it! He had brought Lazarus back to life again, and He had given Martha the opportunity to watch it happen. Martha of Bethany believed in Jesus, the Messiah, the Holy Son of God!

You can trust Jesus to do impossible things. Believe in Him with your whole heart.

Don't hide your light! Let it shine for all; let your good deeds glow for all to see, so that they will praise your heavenly Father.
MATTHEW 5:15, 16, TLB

"Daughter of Abraham"

WOMAN HEALED ON THE SABBATH

LUKE 13:10-17

HE OLD WOMAN painfully made her way up the steps of the synagogue and shuffled inside. She could hardly walk. A crippling disease had struck her long ago and for eighteen years, she had been bent over double.

Finding a bench at the back, the woman slowly lowered herself upon it. She was unable to climb the stairs to the little room at the back of the temple where the other women were made to sit. Jewish men did not allow women to sit with them in worship service.

Twisting her head, the woman craned her neck to see who it was that taught the service this morning. She heard a different voice, not that of the usual rabbi. Her careworn face lit up with a smile as she saw that it was Jesus, the Teacher from Galilee, who led the service. She liked Him! He seemed to truly love the people, not at all like the other religious leaders who cared more about themselves than anyone else. Why, right now, Jesus was smiling, and He almost seemed to be looking right at her!

"Daughter of Abraham, come up here!" Jesus called to the older woman, using an affectionate name for her.

The woman was quite startled. Had He called her? She twisted her neck

around a different way to get a better look at Him.

"Daughter of Abraham," Jesus called again, "come up here."

This time, the woman was sure He had called to her. She was, after all, the only woman present on the main floor.

Getting up awkwardly, she slowly moved to the front of the synagogue, enduring stares and hostile looks from the men.

When she reached Jesus, He touched her and said, "Daughter, you are released from your disease!"

Instantly, the woman felt her tortured muscles relax, her spine straighten, and she stood erect for the first time in eighteen years!

"Oh thank You!" the woman cried out in joy. "Praise God!" she said over and over, tears of happiness rolling down her cheeks.

But the synagogue leader was angry because she was healed on the sabbath. He believed Jesus had broken God's law by working on the sabbath.

"There are six days of the week to work," the rabbi shouted to the people. "Those are the days to come for healing, not on the sabbath!"

"You hypocrite!" Jesus replied. "You work on the sabbath! Don't you untie your cattle from their stalls on the sabbath and lead them out to water? Is it wrong for Me, just because it is the sabbath, to free this woman from the bondage she has been under for eighteen years?"

Then the leader was ashamed and said no more. The woman's friends were happy for her and the people rejoiced for what Jesus had done.

Instead of trying to appear godly, be like God and care for people.

Not all who sound religious are godly people.
MATTHEW 7:21A, TLB

Mothers and Babies

MOTHERS SEEKING BLESSING

LUKE 18:15-17

NE DAY, as Jesus and His followers were walking through a village, several mothers brought their babies and small children to Jesus to be blessed by Him.

Jesus' disciples, thinking that they and Jesus had more important things to do, became irritated. "Go away! Don't bother the Master!" they growled at the mothers and fathers.

But Jesus sat down at the side of the road and called the little children over to Him. He took the babies into His arms and blessed them.

"Let the children come to Me!" Jesus told His disciples. "Never send them away! The Kingdom of God belongs to those who have hearts as trusting as these little children. Anyone who doesn't have their kind of faith will never get inside the gates of the Kingdom!"

Stay young at heart and love
God as a child loves a parent.

*You are to live clean, innocent lives
as children of God in a dark world full
of people who are crooked and stubborn.*
PHILIPPIANS 2:15B, TLB

Salome, Mother of James and John
WOMAN WITH A SPECIAL REQUEST

MATTHEW 20:20-28

S ALOME WATCHED JESUS ANXIOUSLY as He talked to first one of His disciples and then another. A disciple herself, Salome had followed Jesus from the very first time He had called people to follow Him. She and her sons, James and John, had answered His call. Salome had been working up courage for a special request for a long time. It was now or never!

"May I ask you for a favor, Lord?" she said when she reached Jesus.

"What is your request?" He said.

"When Your Kingdom comes, will you let my two sons sit on two thrones next to Yours?" Salome asked.

"You don't know what you ask," Jesus replied. He turned to James and John. "Are you able to drink the cup from which I am about to drink?"

"Oh yes," they replied at once. "We can do it!"

Jesus looked at them in sadness. "You shall indeed drink from that cup," He told them, "but I cannot say who will sit on thrones next to Mine. Those places are reserved for the persons My Father selects."

Salome stared at Jesus and tried to understand the meaning of His words.

191

Did He mean that only God could say who would sit next to Jesus when He became King? But surely God would go along with whomever Jesus picked. Besides, who else was as strong or brave as her sons? Why, they had answered Jesus' challenge eagerly. They said they could drink from the same cup as He! But what did He mean by that?

Suddenly, an uproar sounded among the disciples. News of Salome's request to Jesus had spread among them and they were angry about it.

To end the quarreling, Jesus called them all together. "In the world, kings and officials think they are better than others and love to boss people around. But among you, it has to be different. Whoever wants to be a leader must first be a servant, and if you want to be a real leader, you must serve like a slave! Your attitude must be like Mine, for I did not come to be served by others, but I came to serve people and to give up My life for them."

The arguments ended. Everyone was silent, but Salome saw the looks of confusion on their faces. She was a bit confused herself. How could you be both a servant and a leader? What did Jesus mean when He said He had come to give up His life for other people? Wasn't He the Messiah? Wasn't He going to raise an army and free His people from the Romans so that Israel would once more be a proud and victorious nation? That's what a lot of people thought. Wasn't that what God had in mind, too?

A true leader starts by being a servant.

Your attitude should be the kind that was shown by Jesus Christ, who . . . laid aside his mighty power and glory, taking the disguise of a slave and becoming like men.
PHILIPPIANS 2:6, 7, TLB

Widow with Two Coins
WOMAN WHO GAVE ALL SHE COULD

MARK 12:38-44

STANDING ALONE in the court of the women at the temple, a poor widow watched the long lines of elaborately dressed people parade past the collection boxes. The people made sure that others noticed the lavish amounts of their gifts. The rich, including the self-important religious leaders, dropped their money into the box with great ceremony.

Feeling unimportant, small, and shabby in comparison, the widow fingered the two copper coins she had brought for the collection box. Every sabbath it was the same. After waiting for the rich to deposit their ample gifts, she would follow after them and quickly drop her meager gift in the collection box, hoping that no one would notice how small it was. Then she would bow her head and hope that somehow God would use what she gave Him, though it seemed insignificant compared to the others.

With a sigh, the widow pulled her shawl tightly around her head and hurriedly dropped her two coins into the box. She turned and disappeared into the crowd, unnoticed by anyone but one person.

"Did you see that poor widow?" Jesus asked His disciples. "She gave more than all those rich men put together! For they gave a little of their extra fat, while she gave up her last penny!"

The disciples stared after the woman. Just a few moments before, Jesus had told them, "Beware of the teachers of religion! For they love to wear the robes of the rich and scholarly, and to have everyone bow to them as they walk through the markets. They love to sit in the best seats in the synagogues, and at the places of honor at banquets; yet they shamelessly cheat widows out of their homes. Then, to cover up the kind of men they really are, they pretend to be pious by praying long prayers in public. Because of this, their punishment will be the greater."

The disciples may not have understood that here, with this poor widow, Jesus had found someone willing to sacrifice everything she had, just as He Himself was preparing to do. For it would not be long before Jesus would go to the cross and give everything He had for the salvation of His children.

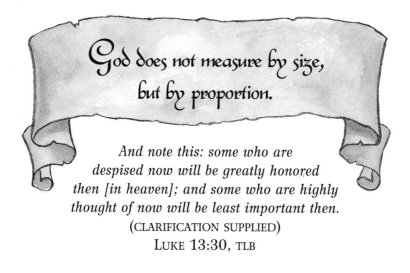

God does not measure by size,
but by proportion.

*And note this: some who are
despised now will be greatly honored
then [in heaven]; and some who are highly
thought of now will be least important then.*
(CLARIFICATION SUPPLIED)
LUKE 13:30, TLB

Mary, Mother of James and Joseph

LOYAL TO THE END

MATTHEW 27:33-61;
MARK 15:22-47; LUKE 23:26-56

TEARS STREAMED DOWN MARY'S FACE as she struggled up the steep dusty road to the hill of execution. Golgotha! It was a hill of death and terror—the last place to which Mary had ever imagined her Lord would come.

The crowd pressed in on her from all sides. Up ahead loomed three large wooden crosses, swaying and dipping now as the men who carried them stumbled, pushed along by relentless Roman soldiers.

Now and then, Mary caught a glimpse of a familiar robe, one she had many times mended and washed with loving hands. Now its hemline dragged in the dust, borne on the back of the one person she loved best in the world, a back now torn and bleeding from soldiers' whips.

Had Jesus not warned His disciples time and time again that He would be betrayed and executed? But Mary had refused to believe it, as had the others, not wanting to hear it, not wishing to understand.

Suddenly, Jesus turned and called out to the women who followed Him. "Daughters, don't weep for Me, but weep for yourselves and your children. For if these things are done to Me, what will they do to you?"

Reaching the top of the hill, the women backed away from the violent activity of men, so easily won over to the perverse pleasures of maiming and killing. Mercilessly, bodies were stripped of clothing and flung down upon the rough splintered wood of the crosses.

With each blow of the hammer, each nail that tore into flesh, Mary sank lower to the ground. She held tightly to someone's hands, whose she could not tell, for the women were all wrapped together in one agonized bundle, their screams so deep that no sound came out of their mouths.

Finally, the hammers stopped and Mary slowly raised her head to see Jesus hanging on the middle cross between two criminals. A sign fastened above His head read: "This is the King of the Jews."

Opening His eyes, Jesus looked at the people below Him. "Father forgive these people, for they don't know what they are doing," He whispered.

The sound of His voice gave strength to the women and they got to their feet. Mary looked around. She saw the Roman soldiers at the foot of the cross throwing dice to win the robe of Jesus. She heard some of the religious leaders cruelly shout at Jesus, "Let's see You save Yourself if You are really the Messiah!" But nowhere did Mary see any other disciples. Where were Peter, James, Andrew, and the other men? Only the women were visible, at the feet of Jesus, where they had so often settled before.

Around noon, darkness fell and covered the land for three hours. Jesus cried in a loud voice, "My God, My God, why have You deserted Me?" Mary watched as a man held up a sponge filled with sour wine to Jesus. Then Mary noticed John, Salome's son, standing beside Mary, the mother of Jesus. Jesus also saw John and told him to take care of His mother.

After that, Jesus said, "It is finished. Father, I commit My spirit to You." And with those words, He died.

A Roman officer exclaimed, "Truly, this was the Son of God!"

In shocked silence, the crowd had come to see Jesus crucified, hoping that God would rescue Him from the cross. Many departed in sorrow and disappointment. Mary and the other women stayed, not wishing to abandon Jesus even in death.

The soldiers came to break the legs of the men so that they would die quickly. It was the day before the sabbath and Passover, and the Jews did not want anyone hanging on a cross during the sabbath. The soldiers did not break Jesus' legs, but they pierced His side with a spear.

A man named Joseph took down Jesus' body from the cross. Mary and the other women followed as Jesus' body was taken to a nearby tomb. Because the sabbath was so near, and by law no work could be performed on the sabbath, the women were not allowed to prepare His body for burial just then. They made plans to return to the tomb after the sabbath to properly wash and cover Jesus' body with spices.

"We'll be back," Mary promised Jesus and sadly walked away.

The darker the hour, the brighter the true light of loyalty shines.

Nothing will ever be able to separate us from the love of God demonstrated by our Lord Jesus Christ when he died for us.
ROMANS 8:39B, TLB

Susanna

WOMAN WITH A SERVANT'S HEART

LUKE 8:2, 3

USANNA HURRIED inside the square little shop located in the merchants' section of the city. Pulling her shawl down around her head and covering her face, she approached the owner of the shop.

"I would like to sell this ring," she told him, holding up a piece of jewelry that had been in her family for many years.

"It doesn't matter if I sell it," she told herself sternly. "My Lord has need of the money."

The thought of Jesus eased her mind. For many months, Susanna had followed Him through cities and countrysides. Calling her long ago, Jesus had healed and strengthened her. She had been with Him ever since, ministering to His needs.

There were other women disciples—women willing to undergo hardship and do without physical comforts for the sake of their beloved Teacher. Besides Susanna, there was Joanna, Mary Magdalene, and many others. They walked with Jesus and ate with Him and listened to His teachings. They cooked for Him and washed and mended clothes, and found lodging at night.

They told people they met in their travels all about their Lord and Savior, helping others to know Jesus as they did.

It was hard, tiring work, but whenever Susanna became weary, she would remember the gratitude always present in Jesus' eyes for the tasks she performed. He never took without giving more in return.

"I will give you a fair price for the ring," the owner of the shop spoke loudly, jerking Susanna out of her thoughts and back to the present.

She took the coins from the man. Now there was enough money to pay for lodging and food for Jesus and the disciples for a few more nights.

Leaving the shop, Susanna joined her female companions as they searched the city for people willing to open their doors to Jesus and the disciples. Then Susanna gave of her money, as did other women on other nights, to pay the expenses. It was a sacrifice, but Susanna was willing to sacrifice all she had for Jesus. She loved Him with all her heart and would serve like a slave on His behalf.

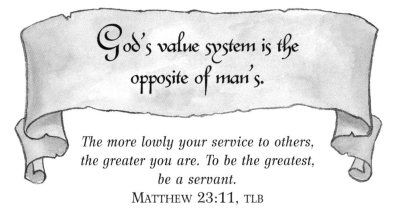

God's value system is the opposite of man's.

The more lowly your service to others, the greater you are. To be the greatest, be a servant.
MATTHEW 23:11, TLB

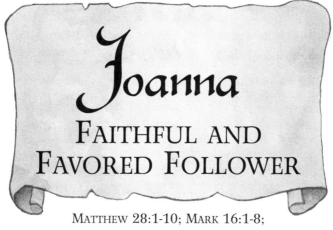

Joanna

FAITHFUL AND FAVORED FOLLOWER

MATTHEW 28:1-10; MARK 16:1-8;
LUKE 8:2, 3; 24:1-11

ICKING UP a bundle of embalming spices, Joanna followed the other women as they stepped outside. It was early Sunday morning. The sun had not yet come up and all was still and dark.

"What if the soldiers are guarding the tomb?" a woman whispered.

"Then we'll tell them we have come to anoint the body with spices," another answered.

"How will we ever roll away the heavy stone?" a third worried.

"Perhaps the soldiers will help us!"

Stumbling along the unfamiliar streets of Jerusalem, Joanna was thankful for the darkness. It hid her grief. She hoped it would be dark forever, that the sun would never shine again! Jesus, her light, the one person she had lived for, the one who had filled her life with hope, was gone and all of Joanna's dreams had died with Him.

Like the other women, Joanna was a disciple of Jesus, following Him from town to town, using her own money to care for His personal needs. She was different from the others, however, for Joanna's permanent home was in the palace of Herod, the Tetrarch, where her husband served as Herod's steward. Joanna had left her home to stay at the side of her Savior. She would have gladly given the rest of her life in service to Jesus. How could He be dead? She was lost now without purpose or plan to her life. She would perform this one last task for her Lord—anoint His body for burial—and then hope for death herself.

Similar thoughts were in the minds of all the women as they approached the tomb that stood in a grove of trees near the dark hill of Golgotha. When they reached it, however, there were no Roman soldiers on guard and the heavy stone had been rolled away from the entrance.

"What does it mean?" they asked themselves. There was no dark feeling of death here, but instead, a sense of wonder.

Cautiously, the women entered the tomb and, suddenly, two angels appeared before them. A dazzling light hit their eyes and the women fell down in fear.

"Why are you looking in a tomb for someone who is alive?" the angels asked them. "Jesus isn't here! He has come back to life again! Don't you remember what He told you back in Galilee—that the Messiah must be betrayed and crucified and that He would rise again on the third day? Now, go and tell the others what has happened."

As she rushed from the tomb, Joanna's heart was filled with hope once more. Jesus was alive! She and the others began to run to tell the other disciples. But, suddenly, Jesus Himself appeared before them!

"Good morning!" He said to them.

The women fell to the ground in fright.

"Don't be afraid," Jesus told them. "Go and tell the others to return to Galilee. I will meet you there."

The women's faces broke into radiant smiles. Their Lord stood before them, risen and whole, victorious over death. A miracle above all miracles had happened, and Jesus had chosen them to be the first disciples to whom He appeared! They had been faithful and had not deserted Him even in death and He had rewarded them with such favor. Joyfully, Joanna and the other women ran to proclaim the good news. Jesus is risen!

Jesus brightens our hearts just as the morning sun chases away the dark shadows of night.

O death, where is your victory?
O death, where is your sting?
I CORINTHIANS 15:55, NASB

Mary Magdalene
First to See the Risen Lord

JOHN 20:1-20

LL ALONE, Mary hurried back to the tomb where three days before the body of Jesus had laid. She was terribly upset. So many things had gone wrong last week. It had all started Thursday night when Jesus had told His disciples that He was eating His last meal with them. Then, early Friday morning, Jesus had been arrested by Roman soldiers and had stood trial before the local religious leaders. Mary had walked with Him to the end, standing near the cross with the other women as the one she worshiped cried out to God and died.

Wrapping the tortured body of Jesus in white linen, Mary went with the other women to lay Him in a tomb. Then, after sitting grief-stricken through the long sabbath hours, Mary returned to the tomb early this morning and found it empty. The body that she came to wash and perfume was gone! In its place, two angels appeared and told Mary that Jesus was alive again. She rushed from the tomb and ran to tell the good news to the other disciples. But the men did not believe her words and thought she was making it all up. Peter and John came to see the empty tomb for themselves, but the angels were

gone and Peter and John soon left. The tomb seemed so dark and empty. Her mind was in a state of shock over the events of the last few days. Oh, what really happened to the body of Jesus?

As she stood there all alone and crying, she suddenly sensed that someone was standing behind her. Turning, she saw that it was a man.

"Why are you crying?" he asked her. "Whom are you looking for?"

Thinking that the man was the gardener, the man who took care of the area around the tombs, Mary said, "Sir, if you have taken Jesus away, tell me where you have put Him, and I will go and get Him."

"Mary!" the man said, and instantly she recognized Jesus.

Rushing forward, Mary reached out to Him, but Jesus said, "Don't touch Me, for I have not yet ascended to My Father. Go and tell the others that you have seen Me and that I shall ascend to My Father and your Father, My God and your God!"

This time, when Mary found the others, she confidently told them, "I have seen the Lord!" She gave them the rest of Jesus' message. Though some were doubtful, Mary did not care. She had been faithful to her Lord up to the end and He had rewarded her for it. He had appeared to her first, before any of the others, and she would treasure that forever in her heart. Jesus was alive! Mary's whole being sang with joy. Jesus is alive!

That evening, Jesus appeared to the other disciples as they met together behind locked doors for fear of the religious leaders. Jesus showed them the wounds in His hands from the nails that had pierced them and the hole in His side from the spear thrust. Then they were all convinced and knew that what Mary had told them was true. Jesus, indeed, had risen from the dead!

Many people boast loudly of their faith, but few really live it.

It is the one who has endured to the end who will be saved.
MATTHEW 10:22B, NASB

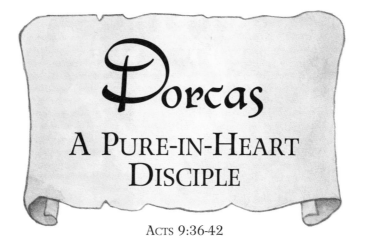

Dorcas

A Pure-in-Heart Disciple

ACTS 9:36-42

"PLEASE TAKE these coats for you and your children," Dorcas said as she handed the poor widow the garments.

"Bless you, Dorcas!" the widow cried. "I don't know what we would do without you. Won't you come in and rest?"

"No, I must get home. I have so much to do." Dorcas turned away.

"You do too much for others, Dorcas! You must think of yourself once in a while," the widow called, but Dorcas was already far down the street.

Stumbling through the front door of her own house, Dorcas sat down heavily in a chair. "I feel so tired," she told herself. That was unusual. Dorcas had always worked energetically from morning to night making clothes for the poor people of the city of Joppa. Along with the clothes, Dorcas would take them baskets of food and other necessary items.

Putting a hand to her forehead, Dorcas felt the clammy heat of a fever. "Winter is coming and I don't have time to get sick," she told herself as she looked at the bundles of fabric and partially packed baskets stacked upon her furniture.

"I have to finish sewing this dress," Dorcas mumbled.

That evening, her friends found her dead, sitting in the same chair, a needle clasped in her stiff fingers.

"Oh, no!" her friends wailed in grief. Quickly, the news spread and the people of the Joppa church sadly gathered in the home of Dorcas.

"What shall we do without Dorcas?" everyone moaned, for there had been no one with a kinder heart or a more generous spirit than Dorcas.

"I heard that Peter, the Lord's apostle, is staying in Lydda," one of the women said. "There are reports that he just healed a man who had been paralyzed for eight years! Perhaps he would come to Joppa and pray for Dorcas."

Excitedly, the church sent two men to Lydda. When Peter heard their story, he returned with them to Joppa. Entering the home of Dorcas, Peter went upstairs to a bedroom where Dorcas' body had been laid. The room was crowded with weeping women, widows who showed one another the many coats and other clothing that Dorcas had made for them.

Peter asked everyone to leave the room. Then he knelt and prayed. Turning to the body, he said, "Dorcas, arise!" and she opened her eyes!

Peter took Dorcas by the hand and helped her to stand up. Then he called in all the people and presented Dorcas to them.

The people laughed and cried with joy. The news spread throughout the city and many others came to believe in the Lord because of it. Dorcas continued her work among the poor with renewed health and energy. God had given her a gift that few people receive—a second life on earth—and she was determined to make it count!

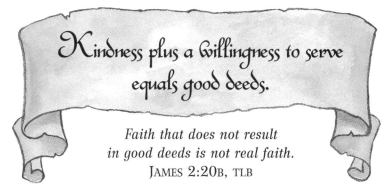

Kindness plus a willingness to serve equals good deeds.

Faith that does not result in good deeds is not real faith.
JAMES 2:20B, TLB

Mary, Mother of John Mark

DEFIER OF DANGER

ACTS 12:1-12

 OME TO MY HOUSE tonight for a prayer meeting. We will ask God to save Peter from execution tomorrow. We plan to pray all night!" Mary hurriedly delivered her message to the Christians of Jerusalem.

For many weeks, they had gathered in Mary's large home for prayer and worship. Mary willingly gave over her house to the young church even though persecution by Herod was now a dangerous threat. Just recently, to please some of the Jewish religious leaders, Herod had killed the apostle James, John's brother. He had then arrested Peter and imprisoned him. Peter was to be turned over by Herod for execution tomorrow!

"Dear Lord, please save Peter from these evil men," Mary prayed. She believed with all her heart in the miraculous power of God. She had seen so many of His miracles. Why, just recently, Jesus had appeared to a man named Saul who once hated the followers of Jesus and had sent many to their deaths. The Lord Jesus had told Saul to stop his persecutions. Saul had obeyed and had become a Christian himself. In fact, Mary's relative, Barnabas, had become fast friends with Paul, and the two were establishing a church at

Antioch. They had even talked of inviting Mary's son, John Mark, to join them!

"If the Lord could convert the religious fanatic, Saul, to believing in Jesus, then He can certainly rescue Peter from prison," Mary told herself.

She quickly delivered her message to the rest of the church members. It was a dangerous business. She could be arrested and put to death for her actions. Christian men and women alike were being persecuted for their faith. They might not hesitate to kill one who used her home as a church.

"No matter what happens, I and my household are Yours, Lord Jesus," Mary whispered. "I will serve You forever!"

Later, when Peter was miraculously freed from prison by an angel, many worshiped God for what he had done.

> Don't be afraid of hard times; instead, use them to measure the strength of your faith.
>
> *Stand steady, and don't be afraid*
> *of suffering for the Lord.*
> II TIMOTHY 4:5A, TLB

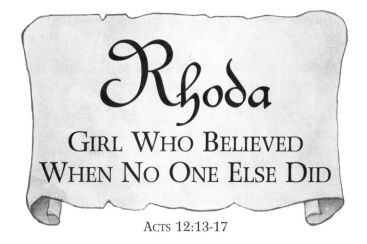

Rhoda

Girl Who Believed When No One Else Did

Acts 12:13-17

 NDER COVER OF DARKNESS, the Jerusalem believers knocked softly at the gate of the courtyard that led to Mary's house. They had to be cautious as King Herod had begun openly to persecute the followers of Jesus. Even now, the apostle Peter was held in prison awaiting execution in the morning. Mary, mother of John Mark, was holding a special prayer meeting at her house to ask God to rescue Peter.

Rhoda, a young servant girl, was in charge of opening the courtyard door. She had performed this task many times before and knew the special knock and secret password used by the church members. She also recognized most of their voices.

Soon a great many had gathered and prayer began. Rhoda joined them as usual, for Mary believed that all in her household, even the servants, should come to know Jesus. Rhoda stayed close by the courtyard, however, to listen for late arrivals.

The hour grew quite late, but that did not stop them. The believers planned to pray all night. Suddenly, a noise caught Rhoda's ear. Someone was knocking at the gate! Slipping away from the others, Rhoda walked silently through the courtyard toward the door in the gate. She had to be careful. If she opened the door to Roman soldiers or Jewish religious leaders, they might all be arrested and thrown in prison with Peter!

"Who is it?" Rhoda asked quietly.

"Rhoda, be quick and let me in!" demanded a familiar voice.

"Peter!" Rhoda cried with joy. She ran back inside and called to the others, "Peter has escaped! He's outside knocking at the gate right now!"

Prayers ended and silence fell as faces turned to stare at Rhoda.

"Peter's knocking at the gate," Rhoda repeated, looking straight at her mistress, Mary.

"Rhoda, that seems a bit unlikely," Mary replied softly.

"You must be mistaken," said someone else.

"No, I know Peter's voice," insisted Rhoda.

"You are crazy!" several people laughed.

"I am not crazy!" Rhoda began to get angry. "Peter is at the gate. It is his voice that spoke to me."

They all looked at one another. Rhoda had always been trustworthy. She had never let them down in the past.

"If it's Peter's voice, then it must be his guardian angel at the gate," suggested a church member.

"That means they have killed him!" people moaned.

"An angel wouldn't knock," Rhoda reminded them. "An angel would walk right through the gate! I tell you, Peter is outside!"

Something in her voice made the others go out into the courtyard. Cautiously, they opened the gate.

"Peter!" they shouted in amazement when they saw it was he.

"Shhh!" Peter warned them. He led everybody back inside and told them how an angel of the Lord had visited his prison cell, released him from chains, opened the iron gate to the prison, and set Peter free!

"I myself thought it was a dream at first, but then I realized that it really was true: the Lord sent His angel to rescue me!" said Peter.

"That's funny," Rhoda told him. "Everybody here thought you were an angel, though I tried to tell them it was really you knocking at the door!"

Everybody laughed. Rhoda looked up at Peter with happiness. She was glad God's angel had rescued the apostle from prison and she was glad that she had been the first to announce it to the Jerusalem church.

Knowing that God will answer your prayers sets you above the crowd!

*And if God cares so wonderfully
for flowers that are here today
and gone tomorrow, won't he more surely
care for you, O men of little faith?*
MATTHEW 6:30, TLB

Eunice and Lois

ENCOURAGERS OF THE FAITH

Acts 16:1-3; II Timothy 1:5; 3:15

S UDDEN TEARS of joy filled Eunice's eyes as she watched her son, Timothy, step up in front of the congregation to lead the worship service. God had answered her greatest prayer—Timothy was a minister of God!

Only God knew the extent of her prayers and how she had prayed continually night and day for Timothy to come to know Him. Eunice herself believed in the Lord God, having been taught the Scriptures at an early age by her own mother, Lois. Her husband, however, was not a Jew and had forbidden the practice of Jewish customs in his home.

Eunice had spent many anxious moments worrying that her young son might reject her teaching and follow after his father's unbelieving ways. But with the help of God, Eunice and Lois had instilled God's Word inside young Timothy's heart and it never departed. Timothy grew to be a man of God! He was not an ordinary Jewish rabbi either, but was one of the very first ministers of the Christian faith, having been trained by the apostle Paul himself!

Smiling at her memories, Eunice thought back to the day when Paul had first arrived in the small Macedonian town of Lystra where her family had lived

at the time. Paul had begun teaching about Jesus, the Messiah. Eunice and Lois (with Timothy) had listened to Paul's message and had become convinced of its truth. All three had become Christians. Paul had taken a special interest in them and had taken young Timothy with him on his travels. The two had become so close that Paul spoke of Timothy as his "son in the faith." Paul had placed Timothy in charge of the church of Ephesus.

A sudden squeeze of her hand told Eunice that Lois, who sat next to her, was thinking similar thoughts. Their long efforts had been repaid today as they watched Timothy perform his duties as the new pastor of the Ephesian church. What a reward for a mother and grandmother!

"Thank You, Lord God!" Eunice whispered and wiped at a tear that rolled down her cheek. Then she and Lois stood with the rest of the church members to sing triumphantly a hymn to God.

Many a strong heart for God formed
its roots through the prayers of a mother.

Teach a child to choose the right path,
and when [she] is older [she]
will remain upon it.
PROVERBS 22:6, TLB

Lydia
FIRST MACEDONIAN CONVERT

ACTS 16:13-15, 40

URRYING through the streets of Philippi in Macedonia, Lydia headed for the riverbank. It was the sabbath and the godly women of the city met at the riverbank each sabbath to pray to the Lord God.

"Don't tell me you're going to the riverbank instead of attending to business!" growled a business competitor as she passed his market stall.

Lydia did not answer but continued her determined pace. She was a businesswoman, a seller of the purple cloth for which the city was famous. And though Lydia was successful at her business, she was different from the other merchants of Philippi. When most of the Macedonian people worshiped the sun-god, Apollo, Lydia worshiped God instead. She had not been born a Jew; nevertheless, she knew the Lord to be the one true God and she, along with her entire household, observed the sabbath in accordance with Jewish law.

Reaching the riverbank, Lydia met the other women. They pointed to a small group of strangers that stood not far away—men from across the seas, perhaps even from Jerusalem, by the look of their dress. She wondered what they were doing here by the river.

"They asked if they might read the Scriptures and talk with us," the women told Lydia. "They seem to be rabbis."

Lydia nodded to the men. Her mind was constantly searching for deeper truth, for more knowledge about God. She would listen to these men and God would give her the wisdom to know if their words were true.

But as one of the men, by the name of Paul, began to speak about a man named Jesus, Lydia was unprepared for the dramatic miracle that occurred within her soul. It seemed as if God Himself touched her mind and gently opened it to the truth about His Son, Jesus, the Messiah.

When Paul finished speaking, Lydia was baptized in the cold waters of the river. Not only she, but her entire household was baptized!

"If you agree that I am faithful to the Lord, come and stay at my home!" Lydia eagerly invited Paul and the others.

The men accepted her invitation and spent many days preaching at Lydia's house and also at the riverbank. Soon, however, the businessmen of the city became angry with Paul and his partner, Silas, and had them beaten with wooden whips and thrown into jail. But God freed them and when they told the jailer about Jesus, he and his household became Christians!

Before leaving the city, Paul and Silas returned to Lydia's home and preached to the believers one more time. Christians continued to meet in Lydia's home. Although there was always the threat of persecution, Lydia held fast to her faith as the first Macedonian to come to Christ.

Keep your mind open and alive.
No matter how much you have learned,
God still has more to teach you!

Lead me; teach me; for you are the
God who gives me salvation. . . .
PSALM 25:5, TLB

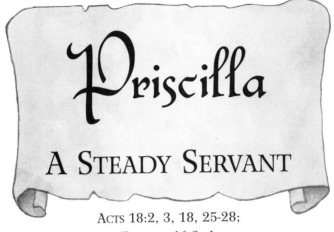

Priscilla

A STEADY SERVANT

ACTS 18:2, 3, 18, 25-28;
ROMANS 16:3, 4

ETTLING HERSELF on a rough wooden bench, Priscilla leaned back and allowed her mind to drift with the rocking motion of the ship. She had set sail from Corinth that morning for the coast of Syria with her husband, Aquila, and the apostle Paul. They had left Corinth when a mob of Jews, angry at their teaching about Jesus, had threatened their lives.

Outwardly, Priscilla's life had been as rocky as the ship on which she now traveled. Roman-born Jews, she and Aquila had been expelled from Italy by the emperor Claudius who ordered that no Jews live in the city of Rome. Tent-makers by trade, Priscilla and Aquila had settled at Corinth and had lived and worked with Paul, who was also a tent-maker.

Every sabbath, Paul had visited the Corinth synagogue to try to convince the Jews that Jesus was the Messiah. Priscilla and Aquila often went with him. Many Jews rejected their teaching; so Paul had given up and began to teach the Gentiles about Jesus. But the Jews remained angry. They tried to convict Paul in court. When that didn't work, the Jewish mob attacked and beat up the synagogue ruler. Finally, Paul had left Corinth with Priscilla and Aquila.

Priscilla sighed. Her life, indeed, was rocky on the outside, but inside it was calm and peaceful for the love of Jesus steadied her.

When the ship arrived at the seaport of Ephesus, Paul left Priscilla and Aquila in that city while he sailed over to Caesarea and journeyed to Antioch.

Priscilla and Aquila labored long in the newly-established church at Ephesus. One day a Jew named Apollos arrived from Alexandria in Egypt. Apollos had heard about John the Baptist and what John had said about the Messiah. But Apollos had not heard the latest news about Jesus. Going to the synagogue, Apollos began preaching to the Jews in the manner of John the Baptist saying, "The Messiah is coming! Get ready to receive Him!"

Priscilla and Aquila heard Apollos preach. They liked his powerful style. They met with him later and told him all about Jesus and what had happened to Him since the time of John the Baptist. Imagine Apollos's astonishment when he learned the story of Christ's life, death, and resurrection! Apollos went to Greece and was greatly used by God to strengthen the church and to debate the arguments of the non-Christian Jews.

Priscilla and her husband, Aquila, spent the rest of their lives in the service of the Lord. They traveled wherever they were needed, giving aid to different churches and teaching about Jesus. They returned to Rome eventually. Paul, in his letter to the Christians in Rome sent greetings to Priscilla and Aquila. He described them as his fellow workers and stated that in the past, Priscilla and Aquila had risked their lives for him, earning not only his thankfulness, but also the thankfulness of all the Gentile churches. All Christians everywhere should thank God for His faithful servants, Priscilla and Aquila, who steadily remained at the task of helping others to know Jesus.

Those who stick to the task and remain steady and true will receive the rewards of heaven.

Blessings on you if I return
and find you faithfully doing your work.
I will put such faithful ones
in charge of everything I own!
MATTHEW 24:46, 47, TLB

Phoebe

TRUSTED DELIVERER OF THE WORD

ROMANS 16:1, 2

HOEBE HANDED the large packet of documents over to a leader of the Roman church. She breathed a sigh of relief. In a wooden ship, she had sailed far across the Adriatic Sea from Cenchrea to Rome, Italy, a distance of over six hundred miles. Through countless rainstorms and high winds, Phoebe had guarded the precious packet sent by the apostle Paul to the Christians in Rome.

Phoebe watched while the leader read the introduction to a letter from Paul. Paul had sent greetings to so many notable Christians in Rome. Phoebe was especially eager to meet Junia, a woman apostle whom Paul ranked as "one of the outstanding among apostles." Phoebe, herself, was a minister of the Cenchrea church, her title given by Paul. Phoebe had come to Rome for her own business reasons and had agreed to carry Paul's letter to the Romans which Paul hoped would help him to enter the Roman Christian community on a future visit.

In his letter, Paul introduced Phoebe as the minister of the church of Cenchrea and his own patron. Phoebe, a woman of some wealth and social

status, had supported Paul in his work. In return, Paul urged the Roman Christians to help Phoebe in any way that they could.

"We are honored to have you here among us," the leader of the Roman church addressed Phoebe. "We will be glad to assist you in any way we can. Thank you for bringing Paul's letter to us. I know it was not easy to travel so far with such important papers."

Phoebe smiled and nodded. As she and the leader looked further at Paul's letter, neither of them realized the importance of the packet that had been delivered by Phoebe. For one day, Paul's letter would be included in the Bible as the book of Romans.

Be trustworthy and do your best in all things for God can make even our smallest tasks into something glorious.

You are the world's light—a city on a hill, glowing in the night for all to see.
MATTHEW 5:14, TLB

Many of the women in this book were heroines in God's eyes. These were women who performed amazing acts of courage and love, even in the face of great odds. These women used their minds instead of their muscles; their hearts instead of swords. If it had not for the courage of women like Shiphrah, Puah, Esther, and Miriam, the Hebrew nation might have been wiped out. If it hadn't been for Rahab and Ruth, Jesus' family tree would have had many different names on it. And who can forget the women who walked with Jesus, quietly and faithfully staying near Him when others ran away in fear.

And yet, not all the women in this book have been heroines. A few chose to go the wrong way and had to deal with the consequences of their decisions. We can learn from their mistakes that it is better to choose God's way than to choose our own.

You, too, can be a woman that follows after God. It is up to you. Only you can make the choice. Will you choose to stand for God and His truth, no matter what happens? If you do, someday you will stand next to the godly women in this book and be known as a true woman of God.

Nancy Simpson

MEANINGS OF BIBLE NAMES

Names of the women given below are those who were specifically named in the Bible. A name such as Woman of Thebez is not a specific name, and therefore the meaning will not appear in this listing. Where there is more than one woman with the same name, the meaning of each woman's name is given in the application in the same order as it appears in the book.

Bible Name	*Meaning*	*Application*
Eve	"life" or "life-giving"	Eve was the first mother created by God.
Sarah	"princess"	Sarah was God's princess. She was part of His royal family from whom God promised would come many kings, and ultimately His Own Son, the King of Kings.
Hagar	"flight" or "fugitive"	Hagar was forced to take flight to the desert and become a fugitive.
Shiphrah	"prolific" (abundant growth)	Midwife who helped Hebrew women bear their children
Puah	"child bearing"	Midwife who helped Hebrew women bear their children
Jochebed	"glory of Jehovah" or "Jehovah is her glory"	Jochebed possessed Godly faith.
Miriam	"bitterness"	As a young Hebrew girl, Miriam must have had many moments of bitterness as she watched her people forced into slavery by the Egyptians, especially when their cruel laws threatened even the existence of her baby brother.

Zipporah	"a little bird"	This name was a term of endearment given to her by her father.
Rahab	"broad or spacious"	Rahab's heart was broad enough to possess faith in the Hebrew God Jehovah. She protected Hebrew spies with a fierce determination to join the right side.
Deborah	"a bee"	Deborah was wise as a bee.
Jael	"wild" or "mountain goat"	Nomadic, Jael was part of the "wild" in which she lived, sturdy and strong as the mountain goats she raised.
Delilah	"delicate" or "dainty one"	To win Samson's heart, Delilah may have appeared delicate or dainty. However, her heart was filled with greed to the extent that she would sell her lover to his enemy.
Orpah	"stiff-necked" or "stubborn"	Orpah was stubbornly committed to her own well-being, and had little trouble abandoning Naomi and Ruth.
Naomi	"pleasant"	Remembered as pleasant, Naomi told her Bethlehem friends to change her name to *Mara,* meaning "bitterness" as she was bitter because of the loss of her husband and sons.
Ruth	"friendship"	Ruth showed the highest form of friendship when she chose to leave her own family and country to remain with Naomi.

Hannah	"grace" or "compassion"	God looked upon Hannah with compassion and graciously gave her a child.
Michal	"who is like Jehovah"	Michal discovered there was no one as strong as God to protect her husband, David, from the murderous jealousy of her father, King Saul.
Abigail	"cause of joy"	Her wisdom and beauty brought joy to many, including King David.
Bathsheba	"daughter of an oath"	As strong as a solemn oath, Bathsheba determined that her son, Solomon, would be king.
Tamar	"a palm tree" (meaning wealth and beauty)	1. and 2. As Tamar's life so tragically reveals, wealth and beauty are poor substitutes for love and a father's care.
Esther	"A star"	Esther was a bright star for her people by saving them from destruction.
Vashti	"beautiful woman"	Vashti believed that inner beauty of the soul is far more valuable than outer beauty.
Huldah	"weasel"	As a weasel consumes great numbers of vermin (mice and rats), so Huldah prophesied national ruin unless Judah destroyed its vermin—foreign idols, altars, and shrines—and returned to God.
Rizpah	"a hot or baking stone"	Rizpah displayed a passion that was hot as a baking stone in protecting the bodies of her two sons.

Jezebel:	"chaste" (pure, modest, decent)	Jezebel was anything but pure, modest, and decent. Her love for wickedness demonstrates how sin can turn noble traits upside down into something evil.
Jehosheba	"Jehovah is her oath"	Defying an evil queen; saving a future king and the royal line of Judah; and marrying a high priest reveals the Lord as the mainstay in Jehosheba's life.
Gomer	"completion"	As Gomer sold herself completely to adultery, so Israel sold itself to idolatry, resulting in God giving the nation over to its enemies.
Salome	"peace" (from Shalom)	1. Evil spoils good things, even young daughters, and whatever peace Salome (the dancer) might have enjoyed or given to others was destroyed by the evil practices of the family of Herod. 2. Salome (mother of James and John) generated anything but peace among the disciples when she asked a special favor for her sons from Jesus.
Mary	"bitterness"	1. Though Mary obtained great joy as the mother of Jesus, the sword of sorrow often pierced her heart as she watched the bitter life of her Son unfold as the Messiah nobody understood. 2. (Mary of Bethany) Though she discovered the joy of knowing Jesus, her heart was filled with sorrow and bitterness as she alone anointed Jesus for burial. 3. Faithful disciple, Mary (mother of James and John) suffered

agonizing pain and bitterness as she witnessed the crucifixion of Jesus, choosing to remain loyal to Him even in the face of death. 4. Mary Magdalene faithfully walked through the bitter fires with Jesus and was rewarded by a special appearance of her Lord. 5. Although the threat of persecution was bitter indeed, Mary (mother of John Mark) did not let it stop her from opening her home to the worshipers of Jesus.

Susanna	"a white lily"	As the white lily symbolizes Easter when Jesus rose again, so Susanna gave her life to serve Jesus and gained an honored seat in His Kingdom.
Joanna	"Jehovah has shown favor"	As one of the very first disciples to whom the risen Lord appeared, Joanna, indeed, experienced the favor of God.
Dorcas	"a gazelle"	Soft and gentle as a gazelle, Dorcas lived her life for others, making her a true "pure in heart" disciple of the Lord.
Rhoda	"rose"	Just as a rose adds richness to a garden, so Rhoda's youthful but powerful faith exemplifies that of the first Jerusalem church.
Eunice	"conquering well" (happy victory)	Eunice and her mother, Lois, imparted an incredible faith in God to Timothy that enabled him to conquer many things as he trained to become a pastor.
Lois	"agreeable"	(See above)

Lydia	"bending"	Lydia's openheartedness to the gospel showed others that she would change her way of thinking or bend when faced with the truth.
Priscilla	"primitive or simplistic" meaning "worthy or venerable"	Guided by the simple rule— serve God by helping others to know Him—Priscilla's dedication earned the praise of Paul and the Gentile churches.
Phoebe	"Moon Goddess" of the Greeks	Although her name was associated with the light of the moon, Phoebe shone instead as a light for Jesus.